Fisherman's Path to Leadership

224 Lessons from the Wisdom of Nature

OLEG KONOVALOV

Copyright © 2024 by Oleg Konovalov. All rights reserved. Except as permitted by law, no part of this publication may be reproduced, stored in a database or retrieval system or distributed in any form, in whole or in part, by any means, electronic, mechanical, photocopying, recording, or otherwise, without the prior written permission of the copyright holder. To request permission, please e-mail oleg@olegkonovalov.com.

Printed in the United States of America.

ISBN: 9798872377399

Kindle Direct Publishing, Seattle, Washington, United States

Cover and interior design by Carrie Ralston, Simple Girl Design LLC.

PRAISES

"The Fisherman's Path to Leadership is unique, compelling, practically inspiring, and a great story-filled read. It might not inspire you to head to sea or pick up a fishing rod, but it will definitely make you think again about leadership and how you practice it."

STUART CRAINER
Cofounder of Thinkers50

"Oleg Konovalov's unique perspective challenges traditional notions of leadership by drawing lessons from the world around us. Through captivating stories and practical advice, Oleg shares his wealth of experience as an executive coach, offering a fresh and thought-provoking approach to leadership. This book is a valuable resource for anyone seeking to enhance their leadership skills and uncover new perspectives on what it means to be an effective leader."

DR. MARSHALL GOLDSMITH
Thinkers50 #1 Executive Coach and *New York Times* bestselling author of *The Earned Life, Triggers,* and *What Got You Here Won't Get You There*

"At the beginning of mankind, tribes read the signs from the earth and the sea and transformed them as learnings from nature for their survival.

In the 21st century, Oleg Konovalov – in his book *The Fisherman's Path to Leadership* – applies this technique of what the huge Atlantic Ocean and the fishing industry, as well as recreational fly fishing, teach us how to progress in our leadership styles of today.

It is hard-earned learnings from stormy weather, a tough working environment, together with salty seamen, but also from special places of solitude and relaxation followed by enlightening insights on modern leadership.

It is truly a continuous learning experience from everyday life and hardship at sea. Far away from schools, MBAs, and academia, but learning made from actions and reflections.

A must-read for those who believe in lifelong learning and growing big, from small insights, nature as a source is offering us!

The book brings me back to childhood and growing in Smaland, Sweden (redneck county), and moves me to the future, with new great insights for my individual leadership development. It is a book with glimmering happiness and written in a spiritual and jaunty way! Go for it!"

STEFAN LORENTZSON
Senior Vice President Communications, CSR, PA and Brand, Volvo Groups Trucks Operations

"In this engaging and lively book, renowned management thought leader Oleg Konovalov demonstrates how what some might look at as a leisure activity – fishing – can have a profound impact on our understanding of leadership and the new world of work.

Oleg's approach to mastering management artfully blends soothing stories of serene river fishing with thrilling high-sea adventures. This captivating combination offers deep insights into the art of leadership."

> ALF REHN
> Professor of innovation, design and management
> at Faculty of Engineering, University of Southern
> Denmark, Thinkers50

"Oleg Konovalov is a globally recognized Master in vision and visionary leadership and a professional fishing expert. In his 'The Fisherman's Path to Leadership' book, he offers timeless wisdom for leaders at all levels. Oleg's decades of experience facing the natural forces illuminate the path to becoming a great leader. His unique perspective offers readers a fresh and enlightening way to understand and enhance their leadership skills.

We are part of nature, we learn from nature, and nature makes us better. Oleg illustrates how the wisdom of nature can be harnessed to become a better leader and reminds us that nature is a source of inspiration and guidance. Whether you are an aspiring leader or a seasoned executive, this thought-provoking book offers invaluable practical lessons and tips that will resonate with anyone seeking to enhance their leadership skills and deepen their connection with nature."

> JENNY M. FERNANDEZ
> Chief Marketing Officer at Loacker, Columbia Business & NYU Professor, HBR contributor

"In his new book, Oleg Konovalov teaches us that nature is the wisest leadership coach available and one that helps us to become better with every interaction. In a deceptively simple, and yet unmistakably profound approach, he shares with us life experiences and wisdom as if we were sitting around a campfire after a day of fishing. If you spend any time in nature, you'll recall those moments when you catch a shadow of something from the corner of your eye, a momentary glimpse, and then it's gone.

Oleg's writing freezes the moment and helps us step back and observe. He shines a light on what is seen and experienced in a way that captures the moment and brings clarity. He helps us slip through the veil of what's on the surface to see a glimpse of what's beneath and within. But he doesn't leave us simply observing. He offers an invitation to join in the journey of growth.

"The book is about mindset and mastery, a valuable, pragmatic, and profoundly insightful observation of nature, self, and leadership. It reminds us that we are connected with everything and are all connected (more than we know). It invites us to step away from striving and toward receiving. With engaging storytelling, humor, and humble self-disclosure, Oleg shares lessons that lead us to discovery, wonder, and a new vision of the abundance around us. My greatest compliment is that the first two people with whom I'll share this book are my son and daughter. Those who will shape the future of leadership need this book."

ROBERT SUNDELIUS
FACHE, Chair at FriendsLearn and TAMP,
Global Deeptech Award Winner

"They say fishermen are some of the wisest people in the world. If so, *The Fisherman's Path to Leadership* is a treasure trove of insights into true leadership. Oleg Konovalov distills his years of experience on the North Atlantic fishing trawlers and his passion for fly fishing into the book that unlocks secrets to leadership success. It is full of stories that make you think and may help you 'land the big ones' in your leadership journey."

JOHN BALDONI
Thinkers 360 Top 10 Thought Leader, executive coach and author of 16 books, including *Grace Under Pressure: Leading Through Change and Crisis*

"A truly refreshing look at the nature of work, success, leadership, and life. Leadership, like fishing, requires patience, adaptability, courage, and connectedness to the environment. This is a must-read for leaders who seek to understand the undercurrents of human emotion and the power of our full being."

>LUDMILA PRASLOVA
>Professor of Organizational Psychology, Vanguard University of Southern California, HBR contributor, author of *The Canary Code: A Guide to Neurodiversity and Intersectional Belonging in the Workplace*

"Dr. Oleg Konovalov takes his readers on a delightful journey, blending deep thinking and fishing trips. With captivating tales and thought-provoking reflections, he imparts timeless lessons on patience, wisdom, vision, resilience, decision-making, and deep learning. Through his enchanting storytelling, vivid imagery transports readers to the heart of each fishing trip, leaving them enriched with wisdom and grace to navigate life's uncertainties. Dive into this world of fishing trips, where patience becomes bait and wisdom the ultimate 'catch of the day' reward. Highly recommended."

>DR. ABE KHOUREIS
>Professor, Ambassador of Compassionate Leadership, Multi-talented Thought Leader

"*The Fisherman's Path to Leadership* is a gem! In this book, Dr. Oleg Konovalov shares his wisdom about what we can learn from nature to become a better leader. Packed with thought-provoking stories and illuminating lessons, it challenges our thinking about how to adapt faster and grow through life's storms. Living in an era of AI we can neglect our connection to nature. This book brings us back to how to be nature-wise and to tap the transformational lessons available in Konovalov's many fishing trips. This is a compelling guide to leadership from one of the world's wisest leadership experts."

SIOBHÁN MCHALE
CHRO, change leader, and author of *The Hive Mind at Work* and *The Insider's Guide to Culture Change*

"Oleg Konovalov took an insightful approach by applying the lessons learned from his earlier fishing job and leadership characteristics. The book is full of real-life fishing examples and reflections on nature, people, and businesses. The book is fantastic by all measures; it is a streamlined reference for anyone who wants to grasp leadership concepts holistically.

I had yet to learn that all these leadership skills could be learned through fishing, contemplation in nature, and interaction with people who share the same hobby.

Reading this inspirational book is a true pleasure."

KAMAL Y. AL-SHIHABY
CEO, Vigilance Consulting, Bahrain

"Why can the cost of a passenger be very high to us? Why should I trust my tackle anyway? What does 'Keep it tight and it will come' have to do with overwhelming pressure? And why on earth should I call the captain when I'm in doubt? What has learning to tie a knot to do with simplicity or casting upstream with expanding the mindset? So many weird questions but so many great answers in this book by Oleg Konovalov, explaining what he learned from the teachings of mother nature he observed while fishing for so many years. He also explains where we belong as human beings and how we can reach our potential as a leader and become a visionary. Simple and short written but full of wisdom to internalize."

>ZEYNEP DICLELI ERDOGAN
>General Manager at Optimist Yayın Grubu, Turkey

"*The Fisherman's Path to Leadership* is an exceptional book that brilliantly weaves together the art of fishing with invaluable leadership insights. This captivating read is a refreshing departure from traditional leadership literature, as it entwines real-life fishing experiences with 224 profound lessons for personal and professional growth. Whether you're a seasoned leader or an aspiring one, the timeless wisdom shared within these pages is an indispensable asset for achieving success. I highly recommend it!"

>FRANK SONNENBERG
>Award-winning author of 10 books including
>*Leadership by Example*

TABLE OF CONTENTS

Introduction	XIX
Part I. Facing Storms to Become the Storm	1
First Trip	3
I'm the Storm	7
Captain's Whiskey	11
Non-stop Rock 'n' Roll	15
SOS	21
How to Unlock the Dead Man's Chest in Three Easy Steps	27
All Hands On Deck	33
Freezing Uncertainty	39
Part II. A Lost Pirate in Waders	45
Don't Give Up When Facing a Loss!	47
Luck	51
Repetition for Improvement	55
Be the Best Version of Yourself	61
Vanity Fair	65
Beware of Passengers Onboard	71

Always Give it Your Best in the Way the Fish Sees as Being the Best	77
Stupid Competition	83
Remedy for Procrastination	87
Part III. Advancing	93
Trust Your Tackle	95
A Lost Whale	101
Catching Nothingness	107
Loose or Tight	111
Passion to Serve Others	117
Doubts	123
Tiny Devils	129
Reliable Simplicity	135
Small or Large	141
Pretending to be the Brown Bear, and a Great Partnership	147
Keep Exploring	153
Part IV. Enhancing Leadership	159
The Most Powerful Tackle	161
Positivity for Success	167
Game of Strategists	171
An Observed Observer	177
Picky Fish	183

Accidental Experiment on   189
Cognitive Distance

Peace   195

Intuition   199

Call for Purity   205

Focus   211

Pause to Win   215

Part V. Conversations Around the Campfire   221

Brothers in Rods and Forks   223

A CEO with a Fly Rod   229

A Fisherwoman with a Great Passion   232

A Top Leadership Expert Casting   236
for Trout

A Solution Finder Who Mediates   238
Even With Fish

A CEO in Waders   244

Part VI. Appreciation for Growth   251

Personality to Explore and   253
Fall in Love With

The Healer   259

Take Care of the Environment that   265
Takes Care of You and Your Children

Putting Rods Away After the Season   269

INTRODUCTION

Days spent fishing are not counted the same as normal life. Fishing makes me feel like a true and authentic human. It reveals the truth about my personality.

My grandfather infused me with a love of fishing when I was five. I've been hooked on it ever since. It's my favorite way of connecting with nature. I have learned from nature much more than from years of formal education. Humans are only a part of nature. We can't create or invent anything smarter or better than nature does. It is an infinite source of learning.

No AI can beat or will ever change the emotions and feelings of a human that is connected with nature. We train AI to think like a human, but we can't train AI to think and be emotional, to be connected with nature.

There is no time for drama when fishing. This is about deep thinking, hard work, and an enhanced mindset. Little thought, nothing caught.

I was always chasing large fish that demanded opening my mind to a greater extent every time. Every fishing trip is a lesson in leadership, strategy, marketing, and personal growth.

I wrote this book intending to share my lessons as if I would be sharing them with my friends whilst sitting around a campfire. My hope is that you will not stop with this book, that it whets your appetite to have your own experience. I invite you to dive into nature and gain practical lessons for yourself.

"

Look deep into nature, and then you will understand everything better.

Albert Einstein

FACING STORMS TO BECOME THE STORM

"

The fishermen know that the sea is dangerous and the storm is terrible, but they never found these dangers sufficient reason for remaining ashore.

Vincent van Gogh

"

Sometimes you need to cross the ocean under a pirate flag.

FIRST TRIP

Back in 1995, I made my first trip as an engineer on a small 18-meter-long wooden trawler, "Sealgear," which means "Sea Hunter" in Gaelic. We went from Aberdeen, Scotland to the rough waters between the Shetland Islands and Faroe Islands, in November, the time of storms and strong winds. Our skipper, Andy Craig was well-known for such trips and had a number of conflicts with the fishing authorities over his navigational and fishing styles. In simple words, Andy was some kind of North Sea goodwill pirate. The crew members were similar.

Six crew members were on board an old ship that was making its last trip before decommissioning into needles, and the main engine had a lot of problems. My role was to make sure that the engine wouldn't die during the trip, help with the trawl, and gut fish restlessly.

In simple words, over these twelve days, I slept a few hours, ate a few oranges, drank many cups of tea, gutted tons of cod, and was in engine oil up to my ears. Actually, facing a severe storm on a small boat is the best detox one can have. I remember vomiting non-stop for days, and still doing my work. If you want to have a good body detox, don't pay money for a fancy spa, get paid for working at sea.

After days of rolling waves, we headed home and could see the Aberdeen fish market quay. The last mile to such an anticipated firm land. And, with a loud banging noise the main engine stopped straight in the middle of the harbor gates. We almost blocked the way into port.

I flew down to the engine room and fixed the problem in minutes. One of the cylinders was dead, the oil pressure was far into the red zone, and a couple of other nasty things. Thanks to paying attention to unusual noises during the trip I was able to locate the problem promptly. A few long minutes of frantic work and a few curses and I had the engine working. I don't know what helped most, the work or the curses.

We made a very good trip in terms of money for the company and the crew and celebrated in the pub. Finally, we relaxed, and I had a chance to ask our skipper, Andy why he goes to sea in such weather.

Andy responded with a smile. "I love fishing in storms when other boats are in the harbor. It means less fish on the market and prices are high. We are not getting salaries; we are getting shares. That means our shares are much greater. We are the co-owners of this trip.

Also, only tough and hard-working guys sign up for such a trip. Lazy people stay home."

I recall this conversation many times when coaching my clients.

LESSONS LEARNED:

- If something could go wrong, it will go wrong. Nothing is over until you are at the shore.
- Tough reality reveals opportunities.
- Sometimes you need to cross the ocean under a pirate flag.
- Professionalism is revealed in facing challenges. Always appreciate and reward them. They are in command of success.
- Confident captain, confident crew.
- Dirty hands always bring food to the table. There are no passengers on board a trawler.

"

*Be a storm yourself that is stronger
than forthcoming challenges.*

I'M THE STORM

We all know about seasickness. In fact, only a few people don't have it. This is normal for all humans, to a greater or lesser extent, regardless if you are a beginner or an experienced seafarer. The only difference is that the experienced know how to adapt faster.

When we witness such incredible instability during a storm, our body and mind read conflicting signals which leads to reactions causing muscles to contract and nausea. Psychologically, if you are afraid that you will get seasick, you will feel sick. Therefore, take it easy, and keep doing your job.

First, I felt sick when facing a force-five storm. Soon, I adapted to a force-seven storm and felt okay. Then I faced something truly fierce and violent – a force-eleven storm. The small trawler, 38-meters long fighting against 10-16-meter-high waves that could crush everything. My stomach was somewhere in my throat, my brain begged for a few seconds of stability and calmness, and my body wasn't mine. I don't remember feeling it somehow.

The distance from my cabin to the engine room which usually was covered in seconds took about twenty minutes of clinging to every wall, handrail, and whatever I was able to get my hands on.

No one and nothing can help in such a 36-hour survival test. We were days away from the nearest safe harbor. The faces of all my crewmates were of a dollar-green color.

In these situations, everyone turns to God.

Yet, before long, I realized something – I enjoyed storms. After the force-eleven, I loved standing on the deck feeling like I was surfing. I realized that by growing through the storms I become the storm myself.

The main challenge is psychological. Growth is associated with enhanced psychological ability. You are either a leader who stands firm and does what must be done regardless of circumstances or you give up and let others fail.

Success is a port you can only reach through the storm. This rough passage demands two key elements – the ability to grow beyond our own fears and limitations and the ability to change and adapt to fast-changing realities. This is an absolutely essential ability to become a true leader.

LESSONS LEARNED:

- Be a storm yourself that is stronger than forthcoming challenges.

- The leader is responsible for leading people into the future. She defines a vision that is much greater than herself and the organization. No one can lead something so huge without the ability to grow and change.

- If a leader fails to conduct his or her duty, the team will fail.

- Change will be painful. The growth is rewarded.

- No storm lasts forever.

- Psychological strength is key for any leader.

- If you can challenge yourself, you can withstand any storm.

- Courage to face the storm is a skill that develops with experience. It doesn't make you fearless but makes you experienced.

"

Leadership is seen in involvement and revealed in care for people.

CAPTAIN'S WHISKEY

Fishing is one of the ten most deadly professions – you probably have seen it on the Discovery Channel. One fishing trawler sinks every third day, and a few lives are lost every day. There is an old belief that seagulls are the souls of lost seafarers, and this is why they follow ships.

High risk is a reason for alcohol being strictly prohibited on trawlers, at least under the British flag. The ocean takes its toll every day, and drunks are likely to add to it. No crew member is allowed to bring alcohol on board except the captain who is allowed to have a limited quantity in his safe for use at his discretion.

I have worked with wonderful captains. One of them is Jack Lilly, captain of "Dorothy Grey," greatly respected by crews and owners, and known for his ability to fish in all conditions. Jack sensed the fish or had fish gills himself.

We were catching a lot of fish with him. My personal record whilst working with Jack was to gut eight tons of fish in a day, while doing my main duties in the engine room and with all the mechanisms on the deck.

A normal day was like twenty hours of work and four hours of sleep. After a week of such hard work, you literally cannot sleep from fatigue.

So, imagine that you are already heading to port right after handling the last trawl full of cod, completely exhausted, and trying to sleep for six hours before the next watch shift. However, as I said, you cannot sleep – your brain and muscles are still tense.

Jack was breaking the rules for the people. He would come into the messroom and pour a decent shot of 'Famous Grouse' to the crew, and then a second shot. After two good drinks of whiskey, you sleep like a baby, lulled by the waves, and warmed from the inside.

Skipper Jack always said at this point, "Thank you, guys! We did a great job! Let's get home without any problems."

Since then, I prefer whiskey. It is associated with warmth and care.

LESSONS LEARNED:

- A good leader shows sincere concern in all conditions.

- Caring for people should come from the heart, be personal, and express great appreciation. No matter who we are, we are all looking for care, appreciation, and acceptance.

- Leadership is seen in involvement and revealed in care for people.

- Appreciating and celebrating people's achievements is a recipe for cultivating loyalty.

- Connect with people by doing something for them, not just saying nice words.

"

You may see the scars that I will get fighting for each and every one of you, but you won't see my wounds. My leadership is a commitment and sacrifice, not a show.

NON-STOP ROCK 'N' ROLL

I tend to push everything to the center of the table whether I'm at home or even in a fine restaurant – cutlery, glasses, dishes, everything. I did this for about five years; it had become a reflex. I'm not alone in this. Every seafarer has this strange habit as a side effect of working at sea.

People love watching snow-white cruising ships, associating them with pleasure and stability. They look like bright islands that nothing could affect. Fishing boats are very different. They are hardly noticed and don't look so breath-taking. For me, every fishing trawler has a tough personality formed by facing unseen challenges. You may hear music from them but most likely it will be the famous sea shanty "What shall we do with a drunken sailor."

To work on these laborers of the sea, you need to have steel nerves and iron character. Fishermen face things that make astronauts sick. I truly believe that astronauts are not trained to deal with adversity as well as deep-sea fishermen.

The first thing I immediately noticed stepping on board my first ship was a strong vibration. It gets immediately through your bones and into your mind – obsessively and constantly. This constant vibration is normal because mechanisms on board are functioning all the time supplying power, and water, and pumping things in and out. A ship is a living body made of steel that pulses like a human body. And this is when we were still in the harbor and the main engine wasn't started yet.

When this few-thousand-horsepower beast comes to life, the fun begins.

We are off to sea. The beast wakes up all other mechanisms where the hydraulic system plays a squeaky solo, winches squeal every few seconds with every pull of a trawl, something metal rolls on deck drumming its own party, and wind whistles into this cacophony.

From a ship engineer's perspective, if I can't hear some of these noises it means something is very wrong. Noise means everything is working as designed.

The weather is up and waves knock the ship around. For a large 200-meter-long cruiser ship this isn't worth noticing, whereas a small 40-meter-long trawler notices every wave. Her bow is up in the sky and then deep down into the water. Way up-up-up climbing against the wall of a wave and falling down into the abyss between them. Up and down, up and down, up and down again and again, for days. We are rocking.

Side tilting adds excitement to this dance. Any cruise ship is designed to tilt by 15 degrees on a side at maximum, and passengers still complain. For a trawler, a side tilt of 45 degrees is a working condition. Imagine yourself being rolled like a tumbler doll from left to right and right to left mercilessly. A tilt of a ship is called a roll. So, we are rolling. Constantly.

Phenomenal conditions – we Rock 'n' Roll on a vibrating deck accompanied by a noisy heavy-metal band. Balance? What balance? Do you feel sick reading this? This is only a psychological reaction. Relax and keep doing what you do as the fishermen do.

Working in such tough conditions is so demanding. Physical strength is important but mental toughness is key. You may see their scars, but they wouldn't show their wounds.

You can't be dishonest with the sea. In the ocean, you need to have a brave soul and have a clear conscience.

This is the way of life for fishermen. Their reason to be at sea is greater than the challenges they may face. Their vision of coming back home with a great catch is greater than their problems.

Next time when you see a worn-out fishing vessel, take your hat off and salute this hard worker of the ocean that brings food to the table.

LESSONS LEARNED:

- Your vision of success must be greater than your problems.

- You may see the scars that I will get fighting for each and every one of you, but you won't see my wounds. My leadership is a commitment and sacrifice, not a show.

- Tough conditions are not an excuse for not doing what you are supposed to do. In tough conditions keep your mind balanced.

- When everything works well, the vibration of your organization is normal. Pay attention to the moments when something has gone quiet. This is an alarming signal.

"

Your vision of success must be greater than your problems.

"

A leader is a dealer of confidence. Leaders are always in demand as people need them and their unique qualities to complement and develop their own. People don't need leaders who feed their stress.

SOS

I made one short trip with an incredible captain, Charlie Newcombe, an old-fashioned, "sea wolf" breed. He was a relief captain as he had already retired but still made very successful trips when he was willing to keep his adrenalin running high.

I came to the bridge, and we chatted about different things and the latest fishing news. Somehow, the conversation turned to ships in distress that sent SOS signals for help.

Save Our Souls (SOS) is a well-known, internationally recognized distress signal when the risk of loss of life is high. Every ship has an SOS button.

Here Charlie made a skeptical face and asked me, "Do you know that saving means a reward to a saver?" – and continued – "There are a lot of cases when an SOS signal was sent without real risk where captains simply gave up without doing anything. For a good captain, in severe cases, when there is nowhere to wait for help, the SOS signal can be read differently – not as a call for help from the victims of the circumstances, but as a signal to action."

Before pressing this red button, think of SOS as "Sink Or Swim." This is about what else you, as a captain, and your crew can do to find a solution. This is for awareness, the action that is manifested in this distress develops from the actions of everyone, and not from the expectation that someone will come and miraculously solve every problem for you. It is your decision to wait for someone's help or to act.

Fortunately, I never faced an "SOS" situation at sea. However, I had a few "SOS" events in business facing the risk of losing everything. In such circumstances, an avalanche of problems falls on me from everywhere. SOS is a great sea term for such an event. Whatever I considered solid fell to pieces, the phones of those who seemed reliable partners weren't answered, and funds melted like snow on a sunny day.

The first reaction is to do what I can. Then the most challenging and dangerous phase comes – panic and helplessness. This is the most dangerous stage where you want to press the 'SOS' button screaming for any help. Panic blocks consciousness.

Here I always recall the captain Charlie lesson. Think before pressing the red button. Is it about true distress or is panic making me thoughtless?

As soon as I calmly analyzed this, I found that it is not my business in distress, but myself. There is always a solution to disaster. There is always someone ready to help when I know what kind of help is needed. People can't help if I just scream without knowing what I need.

In leadership, the "SOS" signal is to be used only when you realistically see a need for it, not when panicking without thinking calmly. Stay calm and confident and the solution will come.

LESSONS LEARNED:

- A leader is a dealer of confidence. Leaders are always in demand as people need them and their unique qualities to complement and develop their own. People don't need leaders who feed their stress.

- You are the captain of your life. Don't wait for a miracle to happen. Utilize all your team's resources. You are a CEO, not a CTO (Chief Trouble Officer).

- Be specific when asking for help. Otherwise, you will end up paying for unnecessary help because of your lack of clarity.

- Panic within a team when in distress is more devastating than the challenge itself. Take care of the trouble-spreaders. Let people calm down and set them to act meaningfully.

- A leader must be a rock and ensure the vision of the prospective future is much greater than any problems. Confidence in inevitable success brings calmness and effectiveness in achieving goals. If a leader is not confident in what he or she is doing, then employees will be even less so. If a leader is confident and calm, employees are calm and confident as well.

"

Panic within a team when in distress is more devastating than the challenge itself.

"

If you can't explain a structure, you don't know what you do. Even chaos has a structured pattern.

HOW TO UNLOCK THE DEAD MAN'S CHEST IN THREE EASY STEPS

One day I chatted with my great friend and co-author, John Spence about our life experiences. John lives in Florida and his book *Awesomely Simple* reflects John's approach to leadership and strategy – if it is simply structured, it will work.

We are both keen fly-fishermen. John loves trout fishing and has troubled fish across the globe, from the USA to New Zealand, and I know a thing or two about salmon fly-fishing, chasing it in the far North.

Only two of us out of a small cohort of global thought leaders have professional deep-sea fishing experience. John worked on small fishing trawlers off the Florida coast, and I was on the North Atlantic trawlers from Scotland to Svalbard and to the icy edges of the Arctic. We both know well how to get our hands dirty and face a storm.

Our conversation came to a discussion on how we gutted and filleted fish on board. This is one of the fishermen's basics. We talked about what knives we used, how we learned the skill, and what fish we handled. John mentioned that he was in charge of all of the fishing tackle on the boat and cleaned hundreds of fish every afternoon when the boat returned to port. He explained that when he was young and inexperienced, the tackle was always tangled; his fingers were always bleeding. Then, with his captain's help, he created a system to keep everything clean and orderly, and be able to fillet all the fish without filleting his fingers.

Here I recalled my experience of learning how to gut and fillet fish.

All crew members are supposed to gut fish regardless of rank, except a skipper. The skipper takes care of the ship when the crew takes care of the catch. I was faced with a bit of shock having no idea how to gut a fish. I made a mess out of it at first. My hands were all over, and my knife and my mind were in conflict. I still don't understand how my mates didn't put a sign – "Beware of a clown with a knife on deck." Then the icing on the cake – a monkfish bit me to tears with her hundreds of razor-sharp teeth. I was about to give up.

At the processing line, I stood next to a deckhand, Toby, who giggled watching me. Toby was such a personality. Imagine a guy that looks like one of the uglier characters from *The Pirates of the Caribbean*, covered by seashells, never shaved properly, with front teeth smashed out by a flying rope, and always whistling some melody. I firmly believe it was "Fifteen Men on the Dead Man's Chest – yo, ho, ho, and a bottle of rum." Toby didn't just use swear words. Swearing was his main vocabulary with a few exceptions.

Once, after discharging fish at one of the small Scottish ports, we went to a pub for a pint where one of our crew took out his dentures and put it into a pint of lager marking it as his, and went to the toilet. Without blinking an eye, Toby took the dentures out and hid them. Imagine the panic and fury of this toothless guy. The crew laughed for hours. This was a typical Toby joke.

At the same time, Toby was smart. He was very good at chess. We had many games and I won only once or twice, probably because he was busy rolling his tobacco.

"Oleg, don't kill yourself. I can't stand this suffering" – Toby leaned towards me and taught me a lesson on how to handle fish. "Think of gutting in a very simple way as dancing – one-two-three-four. One – hold a fish by the head, two – cut the throat for the fish to bleed, three – make a long smooth cut along the belly, four – take all the guts out of the belly by moving the knife from tale to head, five – clean out the remains by the backward movement of the knife, six – throw fish into a fish-washer, seven – whilst the gutted fish is in the air, grab the next fish to gut."

One-two-three-four-five-six-seven. By the end of the day, this rhythm drummed in my mind when I was falling asleep. Fish were flying around me in my dreams. This drumbeat was accompanied by a pain I never imagined before. A former weightlifter, I knew about muscle pain. Here I faced something very different. My wrists were in such pain I thought I was being tortured by the Inquisition.

After the pain settled and I learned to structure my moves, my knife was flying like a butterfly. Some days, I gutted up to eight tons of fish with a small ten-centimeter-long knife while doing my duty as an engineer.

Structured moves allowed me to become as productive as my crewmates – 30 seconds or less for gutting a fish, and 40-45 seconds per fish to be filleted.

The quality of handling fish defines how long it will remain good for consumption or further processing and how much yield will be gained out of every fish. The quality of fish and its weight define the money earned. Therefore, every fish must be handled well.

HOW TO UNLOCK THE DEAD MAN'S CHEST
IN THREE EASY STEPS

LESSONS LEARNED:

- Value comes with structure. Great style comes with structure.

- Actions must be simple and clear as one-two-three-four, thus allowing imprinted mastery.

- Every action must complete a certain valuable part of the process and add value.

- Structure makes hard work easy. Structure makes large projects executable.

- If you can't explain a structure, you don't know what you do. Even chaos has a structured pattern.

- Poor structure of execution leads to poor outcomes.

"

Whilst creating a vision for a business, a leader must envision the role of everyone in a team. Vision is successfully executed by everyone working together, not by individuals defending their own ground.

ALL HANDS ON DECK

We were fishing cod close to Svalbard Island also known as Spitzbergen observing its icy peaks from time to time.

This part of the Northern Atlantic is for those who don't like a simple life. The cold polar winds meet with mild south air causing harsh waves and sending fishermen breakdancing in their oilskins. Luckily, it was August, and the temperature was just above oC, not Caribbean but not covering our trawler with ice, at least.

You've likely never seen a trawl for fishing such bottom fish as cod, haddock, halibut, and coley. It is a long, heavy cone-shaped net that is dragged along the sea bottom. This complicated construction must be checked on every haul, and often demands manual repairing which is not easy on a rocking deck with cold, salty water poured on your head.

The trawl is kept open in the water by two so-called "doors," huge three-ton metal plates that keep the trawl wide-open and physically scratching the bottom of the sea with its "shoes'" or heavy cast iron plates.

These "shoes" must be replaced on a regular basis by welding them to the "doors."

I was an engineer and welding was one of my duties. I was a "shoemaker" every other day. Changing "shoes" at sea is slightly different from what you see in a high-street fashion shop. No one will offer you a coffee or help with a shoehorn.

This three-ton "door" is hung in the air where a few crew members keep it under control by attached ropes. It's like trying to control a wild stallion. It still swings in all directions, and I must try to follow it with the welder. A bit of an acrobatic task.

On one of the wild swings, one of the ropes burst with a nasty sound, and this "door" flew at me. I frog leaped a couple of meters to the side while my crewmates managed to stop the massive guillotine centimeters from my head. Without my mates I wouldn't be writing this book.

Great teamwork is about the ultimate level of trust where we are prepared to put our lives in someone else's hands. At sea, everyone is at risk, and we aim to diminish the risk for each other. We watch out and care for each other. There are many cases where one fell overboard into the cold North Atlantic water having mere minutes to survive and his mates did everything possible including jumping after him and saving his life by risking their own.

Modern trawlers with high automation and progressive equipment still demand the same qualities from crew members as they did decades ago – professionalism, responsibility, and care for each other. Safety is of top importance but care for each other matters even more.

Work on deep-sea trawlers is defined by roles, not job descriptions. We all have core duties and are responsible for everything we do on board and for others. This is about recognizing the holistic nature of what we do together and mutual dependency.

In leadership, the role defines how people support each other and allows them to realize the impact of their work on others – colleagues, customers, and the organization as a whole. A job description is necessary, but it can restrict an employee's vision of the inner life of an organization as one single body.

A job description puts an employee into some kind of box and is isolated from others. Understanding one's role allows a person to see beyond his or her desk to the organization as a whole.

Next time you have fish for dinner, think of the great teamwork that brought that fish to your table.

LESSONS LEARNED:

- A culture of productive teamwork is built on understanding roles.

- Success is achievable when you have an all-for-one and one-for-all attitude.

- With a change in the organization's goals, the meaning of roles may change, necessitating a revisiting of everyone's role description.

- Every newcomer should be helped to understand his or her role at the very beginning of the adaptation period. The aim is to ingrain in employees a clear and meaningful understanding of who are they in the organization.

- We need employees to think and act outside of their mental boxes instead of standing separately as independent units. Otherwise, the organization will remain fragmented and unable to realize its full potential.

- Whilst creating a vision for a business, a leader must envision the role of everyone in a team. Vision is successfully executed by everyone working together, not by individuals defending their own ground.

"

*A culture of productive teamwork
is built on understanding roles.*

"

Most uncertainty is generated by people themselves. Their doubts, worries, and resistance to change feed uncertainty.

FREEZING UNCERTAINTY

The myth of certainty and stability is strongly imprinted in many minds. We claim to embrace innovation while resisting it. In today's business world, people often demand – "Show me something I haven't seen before" and their response to an innovative project is – "How can I know it will work? No one else has done it before."

We are afraid to lose that illusive certainty and tend to ignore the fact that life itself is uncertain whilst demanding certainty at every instance.

We all tend to lose our balance and fall. In normal life, this happens very seldom, yet we all know this unpleasant feeling.

In fishing, falling into the water happens a couple of times or more every season. You can step on a slippery stone, or a strong current will wash you away when crossing a river and swiftly roll you downstream. Yes, that has happened. It's like being loaded into a huge washing machine, with cold water and no washing detergent. If your kids were naughty putting a cat into a washing machine, just imagine me as the cat.

"Lucky" me – I've had the experience of falling twice into cold water on one day and all my gear got soaking wet. Having no spare dry clothing left, I promptly made a campfire and was dancing in my underpants around it waiting for my clothing to dry. Midges had the best feast for years and bears and foxes are probably still laughing about it.

I pushed my "luck" even further by falling through the ice a couple of times. Ice in the Arctic is so thick that it can hold a fully loaded heavy truck. However, fishermen believe that fishing is very good at the time of the first thin ice and at the back end of the winter season when the first cracks appear. Realistically, nothing could happen with the ice still being relatively thick, about fifteen centimeters, which is enough to hold my weight.

Suddenly, my eyes became huge, something that all men have in their pants disappeared, my breath was lost, and my brain managed to produce only one thought – "What?"

I leaned on the ice in the direction I came from, used my knife to anchor myself and slowly crawled to firm land, otherwise, I wouldn't be writing this book.

I learned a great lesson. Later, one of my clients from a nice, warm country that usually has rain instead of snow at Christmas, asked me how to fight uncertainty. My response was, "Imagine yourself falling through ice on a very frosty winter day. What would you do?"

He said, "Oh! This is shocking! I will fight the cold!"

"You can't fight cold, it is too huge, it is everywhere, it is uncertain, and not in your control. You will drain all your energy fighting it and will be dead in a matter of minutes. The only way to survive is to find a solution to get to the shore by ignoring the cold. Uncertainty pushes you to find the best possible solution."

To escape uncertainty, you need a solution that is valuable, pragmatic, and realistic. A solution is a response to uncertainty.

When the future is uncertain, find a solution that will be certain. As soon as you realize that nothing around us is certain, you will change your perception and your mind will start creating that certain solution.

LESSONS LEARNED:

- Don't wait until the moment when life will force you to fall through the ice. Create a vision for life that will be a certainty. Noah knew about the uncertainty of life and the certainty of the coming challenges and built the ark. The rest believed in the certainty of life and uncertainty of possibly coming changes. You know the rest of this story.

- When in trouble, don't waste your energy fighting something that is out of your control. This will only make your trouble greater and make you weaker. Do something real that can get you to the solution you envisioned.

- Most uncertainty is generated by people themselves. Their doubts, worries, and resistance to change feed uncertainty.

FREEZING UNCERTAINTY

- Focus on growth, don't focus on uncertainty. If you feed uncertainty, it will only grow. If you nurture your growth, it will happen. Think pragmatically – all these difficulties and challenges that you are facing are opportunities for growth.

- If a visionary leader uses momentum and sees a point of certainty only as a trampoline for the next achievement, the vision grows beyond observable reality. A visionary leader goes up against uncertainty, again and again, growing the vision beyond even its original aspirations.

A LOST PIRATE
IN WADERS

"

*Pirates are daring, adventurous, and willing
to set forth into uncharted territories
with no guarantee of success.*

Dave Burgess

"

Neither life nor circumstances can break you if you are not prepared to give up. You define when the final whistle will sound, no one else.

DON'T GIVE UP WHEN FACING A LOSS!

Catching salmon may sound simple. However, it is so difficult to get fish to take a fly, and landing it is even more difficult. The fish is so smart and strong that landing one is the peak of adventure. The largest salmon I caught was 16 kilos and it took almost an hour to land it.

Your heart stops when you feel a take, and then... tons of adrenalin rushes through your body. Nothing exists at that moment except fish and a fisherman. The whole universe holds its breath watching this dance in which both aim to dominate and trick the other. A fisherman uses skills and tackle, salmon use imprinted reflexes, incredible senses of every stream, flexibility, and phenomenal ability to resist. It jumps out of the water and dives deep, runs around underwater rocks, sticks to the gravel, and makes sudden sharp turns aiming to spit a hook or snap a line. The fish is a fighter that never gives up. No wonder the number of bites is never equal to the number of salmon landed.

Every salmon fisherman knows how it feels to lose a fish. This is not a loss; this is a tragedy. I've lost many fish, as well as an endless number of flies, and snapped lines are uncountable, besides a few stupidly-expensive broken rods.

I've lost a good number of fish not thinking beforehand about a place on the riverbank that would be the most convenient to land it. My fault.

Fairly soon I realized – don't burst into tears when a fish is lost. Another one is there – keep casting and learning. You may even catch the same fish that you lost in a matter of an hour or two.

Fighting strong fish is the reason why we are hooked on salmon fishing. Those who seek an easy and pleasant life choose to have fish tanks at home.

On deep-sea trawlers losses of trawls is not unusual. Every ship tends to lose a trawl or two in a season. No one cries at a loss of a $100,000 trawl. They keep fishing.

Relax, keep calm, and keep fishing. Your fish will take your fly.

The same in leadership. For some, a loss is like a verdict. For others it's a signal to work more. You either accept failure or buckle down and learn how not to fail the next time.

LESSONS LEARNED:

- Neither life nor circumstances can break you if you are not prepared to give up. You define when the final whistle will sound, no one else.

- A loss is never final. Opportunity is never single or a one-off. Persistence always pays off

- Willpower to continue is when fate kicks you and breaks its own leg.

- Respect and appreciate your losses as great coaches for further success.

"

The extent of preparation reflects your level of leadership, maturity, and accountability.

LUCK

An Atlantic salmon is so clever that I hardly can call it a fish. Salmon is a grandmaster of evolution – strong and smart, it has survived in a cold and challenging environment for millions of years despite humans trying to catch it and pollute oceans and rivers.

Salmon don't feed in a river. It comes into a river purely for spawning and stays there for about twelve months surviving on fat and energy accumulated at sea and then goes back to sea for another four years. It repeats these cycles again and again. Every cycle salmon gains about three-four kilos of weight and becomes more cautious about rivers and possible threats. If you caught a ten-kilogram fish, this means it's her third journey into a river.

Considering that salmon don't feed in a river, there is no valid explanation why you can catch them by fly fishing. There is a common belief that salmon attack a fly because of curiosity to see what is going on around them and are aggressive in defending their own ground. Yet, if it would be so simple, it should be easy to trick a fish. Atlantic salmon fishing is often considered to be similar to lion hunting in terms of its difficulty and demands for mastery.

Many believe in luck. I did as well when I started salmon fishing. Something like – keep casting and it will come. Or, you are lucky to catch one or two.

The more I fished, the more I realized that fishing is not a game of luck. This is a game of chess against a grandmaster of nature. As soon as I realized this, I became much more successful in catching these silver beauties.

Fishing taught me a lesson – luck demands a year of preparation. I became lucky in salmon fishing because every year, before and after the season, in high and low water conditions, in different weather conditions, I spent a lot of time reading water, trying to predict how fish may behave, and even understanding the flow of a stream.

Every season, every day, and every change in weather makes a difference in how salmon will behave and react to a fly.

This is very similar to learning about the market. There is no such thing as luck in business. The market responds to those who are well prepared and know how to approach it. Believing in luck in business is for those who fool themselves and others.

The more you know about the market, the more successful you are, and the better you can lead your business. The less you know about your market, the more you believe in luck. The more you know about people's needs in this market, the more masterful you become.

LESSONS LEARNED:

- Success comes with preparation and mastery which are quantifiable. Luck is a statistical error that is unpredictable and not quantifiable.

- Neither a river nor the market just hands out rewards. Be prepared. Do your "homework."

- Any market is made of smart customers. Approach them with respect.

- Nothing is consistent, including people's preferences. To be prepared, watch out for even the slightest changes.

- The extent of preparation reflects your level of leadership, maturity, and accountability.

"

*Desire to have feeds ego.
Desire to improve makes you better
and masterful and allows you
to lead better.*

REPETITION FOR IMPROVEMENT

Skills are not skills unless honed to mastery. In fishing, either deep-sea or fly-fishing, your level of skill is defined by the ability to fully understand what you do and why, and be able to explain it to others. Mastery demands endless repetition. Repeat again and again. It's not about perfection but gaining that natural muscle memory and full grasping of everything you do.

Quality not quantity defines success. You must do your work well or don't do it at all. There are enough people who will do such work poorly; they don't need another amateurish assistant to do something badly.

There are two key elements of successful fishing – mindset, and mastery. Well, physical strength is important as well, allowing one to walk far and do this physical work in tough conditions. Let me be more precise. The fishing success formula is 80% mindset + 19% physical ability + 1% luck.

Let's start with mindset. Fishing is a game of mindsets, the fisherman and the fish. Little thought, nothing caught. One must be masterful in her or his mindset to outsmart salmon. This is in everything – reading water in different conditions, effortless and precise casting, using the right fly, finding the best spot to cast from, and many other things.

When I started salmon fishing, I was driven by a desire to catch the largest fish in the river. I was banging water with my casts as a woodpecker bangs an old tree. The only difference is that a woodpecker knows what to do and how, and I was just casting. It seems that I became famous among salmon for not troubling them at all.

Trip after trip I fed my enthusiasm that one day that trophy fish would be hooked, yet only a few small fish ended up in my bag. I was losing. Badly.

My casting style was rusty, inconsistent, and demanded a lot of energy. I was soaking wet by the end of the fishing trip. I learned that casting must be smooth, consistent, and precise, and this has nothing to do with physical strength.

Nature doesn't tolerate inconsistency. Fortunately, I quickly realized that my casting style must be silky-smooth, precise, and effortless. My mind had to be in command, not my muscles. If you get into the habit of casting in the wrong way, you will be casting in the wrong way forever.

Fishing demands a clear vision of the environment, water level, pressure, and many other ever-changing factors considered in elegant analysis turned into action. Every element of nature is complex and not linear.

Physical effort is defined not by burning calories and gaining muscles as we do in a gym. This is about being prepared to use your energy effectively, covering long distances walking along a river, being fit to withstand harsh weather and a lack of comfort, and simple endurance.

Luck is something that all fishermen believe in. All fishermen are superstitious when it comes to fishing, and I'm not an exception. They all have their own habits, specific procedures, and luck-bringing things in their pockets. I always parked my car at a very specific place when coming to the river, carried a lucky old Swiss knife in my backpack, and wore the same lucky bandana for years.

Realistically, luck is a credit from nature, encouragement to learn more. You will get more fish if you are good at using this credit wisely. The more you learn, the luckier you will be.

What works against this formula? A famous Persian polymath and philosopher of the Islamic Golden Age, Al-Ghazali once said, "Desire makes slaves out of kings, while patience makes kings out of slaves." Desire makes me active. Mastery makes me productive.

Desire motivates and mastery brings food to the table. Without mastery, desire is unproductive. Desire not supported by mastery made me impatient.

Mastery in thinking, mastery in the physical element of fishing, and mastery in attracting luck comes with repetition. Yes, like in business, sport, or formal learning, it is all about the number of repetitions, whilst exercising patience at the same time. Repetition after repetition and improvement on improvement are the basis for mastery. Repeating for improvement is key. In this sense, every taxi driver repeats the same things every day for many years, but I never saw any taxi driver who became a Formula-1 pilot.

A salmon knows everything about the underwater world and repeatedly crossed the river many times in different conditions. I must be smarter if I want to catch this well-trained fish. So, I must keep repeating and improving.

Every time I came back home with an empty bag I thought, "I saw fish, I had all my tackle to catch it, luck was in the air, I simply lost the mind."

The same in leadership. Leadership is about mindset and mastery. There are no accidental leaders. Similar to nature, business doesn't tolerate inconsistency and amateurship.

REPETITION FOR IMPROVEMENT

As an ancient Greek poet, Archilochus said in 650 BC, "We don't rise to the level of our expectations; we fall to the level of our training."

LESSONS LEARNED:

- Blind desire makes you effective in producing sweat. Sweat doesn't have any monetary value.

- I coach only on something I'm prepared to learn and improve. This makes me willing to repeat and improve more every day.

- Desire to have feeds ego. Desire to improve makes you better and masterful and allows you to lead better.

- True leadership is seen in kindness, humility, focus, exploring, caring, listening, and learning. If you improve on each of these elements, you will simply become a great leader.

- Mindset is the single and most powerful tool for a leader. Improve it every day and on every occasion.

- I improve every day to lead people tomorrow better than today, otherwise they don't need me.

"

*Be your best at what you are best.
This is why you are a leader.*

BE THE BEST VERSION OF YOURSELF

The vast majority of fishing trawlers are purposefully built – for catching pelagic fish that live close to the surface of the ocean, or for bottom fishing, or long-liners, for crabs, for fresh fish and freezers, for coast fishing, and for deep-sea. There are multipurpose fishing boats, but they are not that effective and costly to run.

I know nothing about saltwater fly-fishing or tropical fish. I'm not good at luring and thus, I stick with fly-fishing. I love and know about Atlantic salmon fishing and stick with it. By the way, Pacific salmon is also out of my expertise.

Once, on holiday in Jamaica, I hired a boat for tuna fishing assuming that being a fisherman of the North and knowing a thing or two about deep-sea fishing, I would surely succeed. I was ego driven to prove to myself that I could do tuna fishing as well.

It was a bit of a windy day which wasn't noticeable at the hotel beach. A captain of this charter boat said to me, "The water is rough out there and chances for tuna are so slim that you better wait for the weather to improve."

I was overconfident about my abilities, "No worries, Captain! It doesn't look so bad. Let's go." A few minutes after we left the harbor, I felt sorry about my decision. In half an hour, I was eager to get back, yet still pretending to be okay. In an hour I damned my stupidity.

This charter boat was the size of a life raft of a large ship and jumped at every wave making me incredibly sick. I had no idea how to fish tuna and vaguely understood the deckhand explanation. I am ashamed to admit what happened to me on that boat, so I will omit the details. In simple words, I was useless.

When on returning to the hotel, the concierge asked about the trip, I whispered with my eyes down, "It was okay. Thank you." My ego was kicked mercilessly and left bleeding.

Faking knowledge or expertise corrupts and takes my focus off true expertise where I can prosper most and lead people best. I learned to stick with what I know well and love to do and don't brag about something I know nothing about. A leader is not a jack-of-all-trades. He is a master of leading people and revealing their best.

Leadership is not about pleasing everyone. Leadership is not about consensus. We are looking for consensus when we don't know where to go and what to do. Consensus is a sign that a leader is lost.

Leadership is about firmly knowing where to go and how to get there. If I don't know something or it is outside of my area of knowledge, I will ask experts, not opinionated amateurs.

LESSONS LEARNED:

- What you are good at defines your ability to improve and succeed. Doing things you know little about defines how quickly you will fail.

- Speculating about something you know little or nothing about seriously undermines the credibility of your core expertise.

- Advising on something you know little about is the easiest way to cause harm.

- No one can cast two rods and at different pools chasing different fish simultaneously. Fishing is not a one-time trick but consistent mastery in doing something specific. The same in leadership – be clear about what you are good at and serve your best.

- Be your best at what you are best. This is why you are a leader.

"

You must have a strong and clear vision for everything you do. Otherwise, you will be exhausted for nothing.

VANITY FAIR

My backpack was very heavy when I started my salmon fishing journey. I knew little except that it was demanding. I tended to load my bag with almost everything available those days at fishing tackle shops – boxes with heavy lures, boxes with flies for all parts of a season, countless spools of lines of different sizes, food and coffee for days, and so on. It was enough to survive a couple of years in the wilderness.

I was drained and exhausted carrying it around, yet I thought I was well-prepared. I was totally wrong. I ignored the fact that fishing demands a lot of energy. Carrying excessive things around drains my energy, my key resource. It was pure self-torture.

One day, in a company of similar salmon "almost experts," we were fishing at a public pool without much luck. All of us had fancy expensive tackles made by the best producers in the world. Regardless of the high price tags on our rods, reels, lines, waders, and jackets, the fish ignored us.

Suddenly, a guy appeared out of the blue said, "Hi" and set his rod for fishing. He had an empty bag, a simple rod with a dodgy reel, nothing fancy, yet simple and practical. Three casts and a nice salmon landed. The guy packed the fish, waved "goodbye," and went away leaving us speechless. We saw a magician in action. No fancy brands, no noise, no show. His mastery and simple clarity were a show in itself.

It took me years of conscious learning to get closer to this guy's stage. My backpack became many times lighter. A couple of spare spools of line, a box of flies, matches, a flask of coffee and a sandwich, a bag for fish, a bag for trash, spare socks, and mosquito spray. I could walk easily and have everything at hand and catch more fish.

This clarity doesn't come spontaneously, and only through conscious understanding. Now, I can immediately see whether someone is a mature fisherman or not. The difference is simple – the worse the fisherman, the more useless the tackle.

Professionals use a few handy tools to catch fish and stay comfortable. Their gear works at its best, is never excessive, and is therefore productive. They are about the essence, not trends or showing off.

Novice fishermen will have a heavy backpack, a lot of gadgets attached to their waistcoats they hardly use, and labels, labels, labels to educate fish on the latest sports fashion trends. They travel to Vanity Fair assuming that fish will jump into their hands. Of course, this won't happen, but they will become physically stronger as a result of this weightlifting.

Transitioning from a novice to a mature fisherman, I learned that it isn't the price of the tackle that defines the outcome, but mastery of fishing. My vision for a trip must be clear. Clarity allows doing more with less and focusing on fishing, not on excessive things.

In business, this scenario can be seen all the time. Mature businesses with a clear vision think about how to use only practical resources that would help to add value. Immature businesses talk about resources they wish to have and have difficulty explaining why they need them. Their lack of a compelling vision makes them ineffective, showing off things they don't understand.

True leadership is about clarity about where to go and what to do, not showing what you have.

LESSONS LEARNED:

- Mastery is the most versatile tool that brings the best outcome.

- Every excessive resource you aim to have has a cost that is never returnable. You pay for having it and for stocking it.

- You must have a strong and clear vision for everything you do. Otherwise, you will be exhausted for nothing.

- Value comes first. Without vision, a brand is something artificial. Vision defines a brand; a brand doesn't turn a mission statement into a strong vision. Vision defines that value. If you don't have a vivid vision, a brand is expensive makeup that will fall off revealing the harsh truth.

- Every excess that turns your focus away from your goal harms your business greatly.

"

*Value comes first. Without vision, a brand is something artificial. Vision defines a brand; a brand doesn't turn a mission statement into a strong vision.
Vision defines that value.*

"

Passengers in business drain energy and resources while offering nothing in return. You can't move far with passengers on board. Think how much you are losing by turning your trawler into a joyride ship.

BEWARE OF PASSENGERS ONBOARD

There are no passengers on board a trawler. All work hard and are accountable for their roles and duties. Living cabins are designed for a particular number of crew members, working spaces are limited to specific tasks, food stock is calculated with no waste allowed, drinking water is for sensible consumption, and life rafts are for saving the assigned number of people.

For a few years, I operated a fleet of up to thirty deep-sea trawlers catching cod and haddock in the North Atlantic and traveled extensively over northern Europe. Once, I met a documentary movie producer who was excited by my fishing stories and asked me to put him in contact with vessel owners for making a documentary about Barents Sea fishing. It sounded like a great idea, and I asked a couple of friends who were captains at that time.

My enthusiasm was hit by straight answers – "I'm not a kindergarten to take care of babies on board. If he and his guys are prepared to work alongside my crew, I might think of taking them as apprentices. Yet, this is a bad idea." Another captain echoed the sentiment –

"I will be taking passengers on board when I retire and captain a small joyride boat, somewhere in the warm South. I tried this before, and these passengers only eat, sleep, and make a mess around a ship. You have been at sea yourself and know how things work."

The logic was straightforward – when you work for results, you need all hands on deck, not passengers or spectators.

The approach to passengers in salmon fly fishing on remote and rough rivers of the Arctic is the same.

Once, a seemingly enthusiastic salmon guy convinced us to take him on our trip to a remote river. He had a nickname, Banana, and we had no clue why.

Things looked suspicious when we met at the cars. Banana's bag looked strangely small and light. Fine, we are mature adults and believed he knew what he was doing.

Problems began when we were at the river, far away into the wilds. "Can I borrow your line? Can you spare me a couple of flies? How do you do this? Oops, I have only one sandwich and forgot to take a food container from the fridge. Guys, who have spare socks? Let me fish at your spot while you're having a break." Banana was a passenger not contributing to the trip at all.

At the end of the trip, Banana fell into the water and managed to burn a big hole in his trousers while drying them over a campfire. We didn't know whether to laugh at him or to cry being sad about an almost wasted trip. Here we understood why his nickname is Banana. The guy is nice, but not to be taken on board.

Ernest Hemingway, a famous American novelist, Noble Prize winner, and fisherman known for his trophy marlins stated, "Never go on trips with anyone you do not love."

Fishing is not an all-inclusive holiday. All should work thoughtfully and hard, contributing to the result for all to enjoy.

Thinking about corporate silos or corporate passengers, I always recall a brilliant joke by Jerome K. Jerome, an English writer and humorist from his *Three Men in a Boat (To Say Nothing of the Dog)*, "I like work; it fascinates me. I can sit and look at it for hours." This is typical of passengers.

Many organizations tolerate passengers at the cost of performance and even success. Passengers who are not subscribed to a powerful, meaningful, and moving vision are often tired and exhausted. They avoid any genuine effort to engage and only pretend or imitate involvement. They deplete, drain, and diminish those around them with negativity, disbelief, indifference, and self-doubt.

A lot of resistance comes from office silos at all levels. They have a clear understanding that they wouldn't survive in case of serious change.

They make a lot of noise to show how busy they are and are not prepared to leave their comfort zone even under the threat of being run over by change. They are passengers or joyriders. I think that if someone would produce sprays with artificial work sweat with scents like "Monday rush," "Wednesday improvement," "Friday to-do," or "Annual report hassle," they would be wildly popular among office silos.

LESSONS LEARNED:

- Passengers want a show, not work. He or she multiplies trouble because of their demotivating impact on others.

- A leader shouldn't be surprised by growing office silos and a lack of initiative and creativity if he or she lacks decision-making capacity. This is a result of his or her weak leadership.

- Passengers in business drain energy and resources while offering nothing in return. You can't move far with passengers on board. Think how much you are losing by turning your trawler into a joyride ship.

- Passengers jump at the table to eat first, and off for work last. If you accept passengers on board, be prepared to do their part of the work and be satisfied with a low outcome.

- Passengers are permitted on board with the captain's permission only. Corporate passengers are tolerated in a team with a leader's acceptance only. Who pays for their joyride and demotivating attitude?

> To what extent a leader understands people and their needs defines his level of leadership.

ALWAYS GIVE IT YOUR BEST IN THE WAY THE FISH SEES AS BEING THE BEST

Her Majesty Salmon anticipates royal service and attention. You wouldn't catch much being disrespectful to it. You can encourage or motivate salmon to take a fly but you can't force it.

Like every novice fly fisherman, I assumed it would be fierce competition among fish as soon as my beautiful factory-made fly hit the water. Something was wrong with the fish, not with my assumptions. Yet, it didn't work.

One day, I was blessed with true luck. I went fishing with seventy-five-year-old Alex who had been fishing for decades and knew every stone on every river.

We stayed not far away from each other, and I tried to copy everything he was doing. Alex caught two nice salmon. I had none, not even a touch. At the score of 3:0, we took a break for tea.

Alex was stingy with words and waved me to show him my box of flies. Here a waterfall of sarcasm flooded out. I will leave slang and swearing out at the cost of making this story about ten times shorter.

"These flies are good if you are relying on luck. It will make fish curious but wouldn't make it take. A salmon sees things differently looking at the objects in the water from down up, whereas a human looks at a fly from top to down. You can't see the motion of a fly in a stream in the way salmon see it. Your flies are flat and slim. They need volume."

"Colors are important to an extent, yet the volume and shape of your fly is more important. Fish see colors differently from humans. Her decision to attack a fly is based on how a fly looks aggressive and live, not how fancy it is."

"Don't cast straight under the nose of a fish. Cast smoothly giving a bit of distance to a fly to take the best position naturally. Salmon won't respond to half-measures. Give salmon your best."

Here I realized that salmon laughed at a fly I believed was a killer. Fish ignored my attempts to approach them closely. I had to think of how the fish saw my fly. Not how I saw it.

It was a great lesson from Alex to rethink how I fish.

Success in salmon fishing is based on reverse engineering logic – what do fish want? What are they irresistibly curious about? We see a beautiful fly. Not whether the fish sees an insect, or little fly, or something attractive or threatening in her understanding and grabs a fly or not. I was spooking the fish instead of motivating it to take the fly.

True leadership and visionary leadership are based on the same reverse engineering. Many leaders tend to ignore what is important for people, or what they see as valuable, what makes them engaged, and what truly inspires them. This is all about the value created for people, not for a leader or how a leader sees things. The same about customers. Without understanding people's needs, your business will fail.

This is about stimulus and response to it. Stimulus is what we offer people as valuable. Whose pain do you want to solve? What is the value for people in your vision? How does it answer people's deep desires?

Like in fishing, where salmon ignores the wrong fly, a stimulus without response is just a stimulus. People won't respond to something not good for them. The value of stimulus defines how promptly people respond to it. If it is valuable for them, they respond promptly. If not, your stimulus is left ignored.

LESSONS LEARNED:

- How valuable your offering is for people is defined by their response, not your assumptions. If they see your leadership as valuable, they will be by your side. If not, they will walk away.

- A visionary leader sees what others don't see. However, a leader must see what and how people see, otherwise he or she is totally disconnected from them.

- To what extent a leader understands people and their needs defines his level of leadership.

- You can't ask a fish what it wants. You can ask people what they need and want. In this sense, a leader is in an advantageous position. If you don't use this opportunity, then step out.

"

You can't ask a fish what it wants. You can ask people what they need and want. In this sense, a leader is in an advantageous position. If you don't use this opportunity, then step out.

> A true leader is a specialist in serving his or her own people, not a scavenger of someone else's success.

STUPID COMPETITION

I came to a pool with a few fishermen already standing knee-deep in the water. It is a common-sense rule and a courtesy to others to take a spot further upstream if you come later. The reason is the firstcomers are taking positions downstream and have a higher chance to meet fish that swim against the stream.

I quickly caught a nice fish. Suddenly, a guy who stood downstream at a fair distance yelled to me that it was a fish he had been chasing for a long while. Strange, the fish I caught was out of his reach. I simply ignored him.

A few minutes later, someone downstream caught a ten-kilo fish. At this moment, that guy threw his rod on the bank in anger, almost breaking this precious tackle.

Later, he hooked a fish and played with it for a short while before it escaped the line. That was his breaking point and he quit.

Unfortunately, I have seen many times eyes full of envy in people who came to compete, not to catch their fish.

We allow our minds to be flooded with envy and get drowned in negativity. Envy is anguish over someone else's happiness. Envy and anger over someone's success makes you smaller and leaves you devastated. Acceptance and appreciation allow space for new capacities and achievements. You will get nothing if you don't value what you have.

There are no winners or losers when we interact with nature. Fishing isn't about finding who is better. Nature will decide on this, and fish will be the judge. Similarly, it is employees and customers who determine who the best leader is. Focus on what you can do best and the most value you can create for others, and you will stand out from the competition.

Competition is a choice, not a necessity. Competition only drains your resources and limits your thinking by what others do and not what you can do. Getting into a rat race of copy-pasting what others do without understanding how others think is a recipe for failure. The leader, entering into competition, loses the path of progress, learning, and development.

I'm in interaction with nature, not in competition with others. I'm to serve my people, not to be in competition for praise and rankings. The only competition I'm in as a leader is for people's hearts.

Take care of finding your fish. Take care of winning the hearts and minds of your people. Don't worry about what everyone else is doing.

LESSONS LEARNED:

- It is difficult to foresee the outcome of competition but easy to predict the consequences. There is no competition in leadership, only a contest for improvement.

- A true leader is a specialist in serving his or her own people, not a scavenger of someone else's success.

- Regardless of rank, a leader's ability to focus on people under his or her leadership defines success.

- Don't be a victim of stupid competition. This will only feed your ego, undermining the core meaning of leadership. Such leaders fail to stimulate loyalty, effort, or even simple sympathy.

- In business, the real outcome is in what a team achieves, not in how much better or worse we have done compared to the competitors. They have their own shareholders to report to and their own people to keep satisfied.

"

Vision is the best remedy for procrastination that infuses you with energy and inspiration to act regardless of challenges.

REMEDY FOR PROCRASTINATION

A two- or three-day fishing trip is better than any fancy retreat at a five-star hotel, for me, at least. On one such trip, I blazed far into the wilds anticipating a good catch and tranquil solitude. The weather was nice with a few small clouds.

After walking for almost two hours to that secret pool, I was fairly exhausted and my thoughts were not about setting up camp, putting the tent up, and preparing logs for the campfire. I was already fishing in my mind. What could go wrong? The weather was nice, and the fish were there waiting for me. I assumed that everything would be fine, and I would take care of everything afterward. However, as Travis Dane, a character in the famous movie, *Under Siege* 2, played by Eric Bogosian, sharply stated, "Assumption is the mother of all fuckups."

The Arctic is a place of constant and sharp changes and experiencing four seasons in one day is nothing unusual. In a couple of hours, the wind picked up and the sky turned from bright to grey and then to dark stormy colors. Stupid me, I ignored these signs and continued fishing. Procrastination took its toll. Shortly, it was raining cats and dogs.

I rushed back to my camp. Everything was soaking wet. Putting the tent up took moments, but making a fire from wet logs in the rain was impossible. Shivering in the tent and blaming myself for procrastination didn't make me feel better. I don't want to mention my dances drying my gear and setting the camp again after the rain, and not fishing, of course.

Fishing in the Arctic doesn't tolerate procrastination. Everything must be done in a timely fashion, otherwise consequences could be costly.

When fishing, nothing can wait. Changing a fly later or casting to a promising spot later or, making a campfire later is like waiting for a fish to jump into your bag. Never happens.

I crucified myself many times for spotting fish at the nearby pool and assuming that I would fish there later, on the next trip. It was wrong – the fish was gone without leaving a note where to find it.

Schools of fresh-from-the-sea salmon come with the tides. If you miss a tide time, you miss the opportunity to fight the strongest fish and will have to wait for the next tide in twelve hours, if you have the time.

Fishing is about "go-to" not "wait-again" and making the most of every opportunity. Inaction is penalized by an empty bag. The Arctic doesn't forgive procrastination. In this sense, I love Winston Churchill's saying, "I never worry about action, but only inaction."

Success in fishing depends on ownership of the moment. You must be ready to explore the opportunities given or even create such moments by acting. You must be responsive.

We are living in a time of the fastest changes humanity has ever faced and we must be responsive to changes and use opportunities where possible. In modern leadership, procrastination is a deadly sin taking you off the game instantly.

We procrastinate when we don't know what to do or how to do something. This is a normal human reaction. Tapping into something unknown with no knowledge or information is always difficult. We have solid knowledge about the past, we have enough information about the present, and we have no knowledge or information about the future. The future is yet to be created out of weak signs and clues.

At the same time, many leaders have so-called mind lag, thinking too much about the past, a bit about the present, and very little about the future. No one hooks the future with thoughts cast into the past.

A remedy for procrastination in the face of uncertainty is a strong and compelling vision. Vision is our aspiration for the future that we strive to make a reality today. A strong and compelling vision is the only certainty in this forthcoming uncertainty.

LESSONS LEARNED:

- If you don't know what to do, think about what you can do.

- Taking time to think through an unknown is good. Waiting to act on something known is not okay.

- No one becomes stronger or younger being in lethargic sleep. No one became successful waiting for a miracle to happen.

- Vision is the best remedy for procrastination that infuses you with energy and inspiration to act regardless of challenges.

- A procrastinating leader is an incompetent leader who projects doubts on his or her team. People quickly see this as a sign of blind leadership.

"

A procrastinating leader is an incompetent leader who projects doubts on his or her team.

ADVANCING

"

Progress is impossible without change, and those who cannot change their minds cannot change anything.

George Bernard Shaw

"

If an idea represents a vision at the beginning, the quality of its execution represents how the vision is turned into a reality.

TRUST YOUR TACKLE

If I don't trust my tackle, it will fail at the most inappropriate moment leaving me with empty hands. This is not about how expensive but about how reliable my tackle is. Its reliability is defined by me.

Every element that I buy from a shop must be checked and tested in action. The aim is to be sure that my tackle is reliable and versatile as one effective piece consisting of a few parts.

A new, well-promoted treble tube hook came on the market, and I bought a couple of boxes of a different size. I use such hooks for heavy tube flies at the beginning of a season when large salmon swim along the very bottom of the river.

Large fish demand large and super strong hooks. Yet, I had a feeling that these trebles were not to expectations. The first fish was hooked and straight off after a couple of minutes of being under pressure. Hmm…did I lose the fly? The tube fly was okay itself; the treble hook was bent straight as a mini trident.

I put on a new treble hook from the same box and kept fishing. Shortly after, the same thing happened again. The same scenario with the same straightened hook.

I fished at the right spot, at the right depth, with a very appealing tube fly. The little, yet essential element, the hook, was unreliable. I failed. A guy who was fishing nearby asked what happened, looked at me, and noted, "You must trust your tackle."

I lost two large salmon because of the poor-quality hooks. In fact, this is a totally wrong assumption. I didn't trust my tackle initially and shouldn't have fished with it to begin with.

Yet, some people suspiciously assume that such things happen because I didn't trust my tools and thus, they fail me. Good try, but neither in fishing nor in leadership should unreliable tools be used. If I have a gut feeling that something could fail, then I must listen to it and run an extra test. In the case of these faulty treble hooks, I failed to test them at home having a gut feeling that they were faulty. Purely my mistake.

In leadership, unreliable tools will fail a leader and his or her people as well. This is relevant to skills as well. If a leader is not confident in his or her skills and tools, he or she will fail.

Preparation and testing begin at home. Today, many people neglect to do homework. They come for an important meeting completely unprepared and fail while blaming others. They fail by using the wrong leadership tools and blame wrongly positioned stars in the sky.

Great leadership depends on quality of execution. Whatever a good leader does is to be done with quality.

A leader sets quality standards and metrics for everything his or her team does. Without clear and vision-centered metrics, the whole journey is a pure gamble. It is impossible to reach a destination without knowing what it is. Metrics show the destination and quality standards show your progress towards it. Therefore, metrics must be set clearly and accepted by all involved.

If execution fails to deliver quality, then metrics can't be met. If metrics are doubtful, then quality will suffer. If execution shifts focus away from the desired metrics, then no report can hide it. This is a signal that your team has lost its direction and must be realigned with the vision.

LESSONS LEARNED:

- Trust your skills and trust your tools before thinking of an outcome. One of the things that's a common mistake in launching a venture or launching an initiative is we don't have an agreed sense of quality.

- If an idea represents a vision at the beginning, the quality of its execution represents how the vision is turned into a reality.

- If you set metrics not supported by values, people won't commit to the vision. Without metrics that resonate in minds and hearts, people will only feign commitment and enthusiasm.

- Setting metrics is not about educated guesses, but about being precise as you can't afford even a slight deviation from the goal.

- Without good metrics and the ability to read them, there is no way to determine how much actual progress is being made.

"

If you set metrics not supported by values, people won't commit to the vision. Without metrics that resonate in minds and hearts, people will only feign commitment and enthusiasm.

"

Fear is a normal human reflex. Courage is a skill that can be developed. Courage is acting and thinking boldly in the face of something unexplored, huge, and complicated.

A LOST WHALE

A fish caught makes me happy. A fish lost still makes me happy, just with a pinch of disappointment.

Something strong took my fly and pulled the line down into the deep pool like a nuclear submarine diving deep. How can something so huge fit into a small river? After about fifteen minutes of maneuvering underwater, this monster broke the surface and showed its shiny top fin and tail, then went deep down again. After a few full laps around the pool and a few bruises on my fingers made by the screeching reel, it came to the surface again showing its strong body. This salmon was more than twenty kilos and filled with the energy of a small nuclear reactor. She looked at me curious about what kind of a fisherman she caught today, snapped a fly and elegantly waved her tail "bye."

Back home I shared this drama with my family. Of course, it was a fish the size of a dolphin. After I calmed down with a shot of whiskey, I reevaluated my view – it was a whale, at least, just a river breed.

A few trips later, something similar happened again. A whooping pull, and a feeling of fishing for a submarine. This time, I didn't even see the salmon. The fish ran about two hundred meters upstream, crossed the rapids into the next pool, sharply turned around, and then dragged me a few hundred meters downstream. She pulled the line off the reel and played with me like a puppet. I lost my breath running around trying to get it under control, but nothing worked. This time I didn't even get a kiss goodbye.

If at first I was overexcited thinking how great a fisherman I am, this time I blamed myself mercilessly. This was a one-time chance to catch an incredible fish that I didn't manage to keep under control.

The first time I speculated on my illusive projection of how big the fish was and feeding my ambitions, whereas the second time I was evaluating my capacity to handle such a large fish.

Hearing similar stories from others, I gradually noticed the pattern – successful guys garnish their stories with disappointment about themselves, whereas novices get overexcited about their abilities.

What lies behind these different reactions when a huge fish says, "Boo?" I talked to my friends with similar experiences and found two interesting feelings shared by all.

The first one is fear. Actually, a twofold fear.

The fear of facing something big and strong could be shocking. I want to catch a large fish but am afraid to land it. This makes me think if the fish was so huge, why not thank God for getting me away from the fish?

This kind of fear comes when we are not prepared as fishermen or as leaders. It makes us do something we regret after. We give up without even fighting for something possible to achieve. Success is never big; this is us being too small and unprepared to have it. This was the reason behind losing that second large fish. I wasn't mentally capable of managing such a large fish.

Fear makes you weaker and your counterparty stronger.

The second one is the fear of not knowing what to do with success. We all want to catch a huge fish or execute a huge project, but we don't know what to do with it when it comes. Often, we are afraid of the success that we aim to achieve. I always ask my clients – What would you do with your success? We are good at fighting to the end when we know what we gain out of it and what could be done further.

However, if we realize that the success which is almost at our fingertips is too big, we lose control as our mind says "no" to it. Our mind is not prepared and we are often not prepared to lead this desired success.

Fear of success blocks us when we almost reach the desired success. Always know what to do with the success you aim to achieve. Otherwise, your mind will play against you.

Illusions cloud minds. They feed you with unrealistic expectations – good or bad. This happened to me with that first fish. In my mind, I was already weighing the fish when I should have been focused on landing it. The fish that is not in a bag can't be weighed and cooked. Something that wasn't executed can't be measured and is mere speculation.

Empty projection might feed your ambitions but wouldn't impress anyone with the outcome. Be realistic, not illusive.

Fear and illusion have big eyes. However, don't be afraid of the opportunities you were looking for or brag about illusive projections. Go, try, learn, and win. Your fears and illusions will disappear through the fights.

LESSONS LEARNED:

- In fishing, nature is the fairest and strictest arbiter of who wins and who loses. In leadership, the outcome will show whether you won or need to improve.

- Fear is a normal human reflex. Courage is a skill that can be developed. Courage is acting and thinking boldly in the face of something unexplored, huge, and complicated.

- Illusive projections make people stop and wait for success, taking it for granted. This is not forgivable in leadership. Illusions are for amateurs.

- What will you do with the success you aim to achieve? Be clear, otherwise, you won't achieve it.

- The greater your leadership abilities, the greater the confidence of your team to execute something big, and fear is diminished and becomes easily manageable.

"

If you are not investing in learning about your potential market, no one will invest in you. Optimism is a good indicator but is hardly investable.

CATCHING NOTHINGNESS

At the beginning of my second salmon season, I felt mature enough to do things in my own way. I had already caught a few fish and firmly believed that I could figure out where and how to fish it.

With the season-opening being announced, I went to the lower part of the river to find it crowded. It looked like the entire fly fishermen population was there densely occupying every possible spot.

"No. This is not good for me. I will be smarter and will go far upstream," I thought. I walked a few kilometers along the river by wet banks and took barriers of windfalls with a heavy backpack.

I found an amazingly promising pool with a superb casting spot and unpacked my rod. A few hours of casting and a few flies being lost to underwater stones brought me nothing but disappointment.

"Hi! Do you have a license?" – a fish inspector appeared from nowhere and smiled at me. I confidently responded – "Of course! Let me walk out of the water and I will show it."

"No need. I was just curious to ask. Actually, I'm not checking the licenses of strange guys," the inspector smiled.

"What do you mean? Did I do something wrong?" I responded, puzzled.

Here this old, experienced inspector opened my eyes, "Salmon will be at this part of the river in about two weeks' time, not earlier. But you give a good wash to your flies." Thanks to the fish inspector for being delicate and not calling me "an idiot."

I walked back to the car totally ashamed and physically exhausted. My frustration kept my legs moving. Literally, I was fishing where there were no fish. Salmon gradually fill the pools from downstream to upstream and they weren't there yet. I caught myself in a catch-22 situation – no catch because of no fish.

A double shame was that I didn't even think that this is similar to the markets that don't appear in one day and need to be filled up with demand. I was offering where there was no demand. Or, in business terms, the market wasn't formed yet. Alexandre Dumas in his "Bêtise" (Stupidity) was probably thinking about me when stating – "One thing that humbles me deeply is to see that human genius has its limits while human stupidity does not."

Many young leaders tend to make mistakes about markets, startups in particular.

Catching nothing is one of the costliest activities that a business can do. The outcome is nil, resources and time are wasted, and the energy is drained.

This fishing trip taught me about strategy and marketing in a very digestible form.

LESSONS LEARNED:

- Don't start if you don't know your market. Think first about what people need and in what form.

- Enthusiasm for creating something out of nothing must be well supported by an understanding of the forthcoming changes.

- If you are not investing in learning about your potential market, no one will invest in you. Optimism is a good indicator but is hardly investable.

- A very small share of the active market is much better than control over an empty market, unless you can form it quickly.

"

Give yourself tolerance at the margins. As a leader, give your people even greater tolerance at the margins. We are only humans.

LOOSE OR TIGHT

All novice fly fishermen tend to repeat the same mistake again and again. Mature fly fishermen still repeat the same mistakes from time to time. These mistakes cost them a lost fish and even tackle. I'm not an exception and was good at making a particular mistake over and over again, consciously at the beginning and unconsciously later.

There is a saying among fly fishermen, "Keep it tight and it will come." Salmon is so strong that one can break a line or get off a fly in a split second if they feel any slack in the line. The fisherman aims to keep a tight connection with a hooked fish and control it. Every slack in the line gives this powerful and canny fish a chance to do something unpredictable. A little slack, which is too tiny in human's understanding could be of a fish length and enough for the fish to maneuver and get in control of a fight. A five-kilo salmon could easily break a ten-kilo-strength fishing line without any hesitation.

At the same time, we must give room for the fish to run around and get tired. Therefore, fishing rods are made strong, flexible, and resilient. All reels have drag systems to regulate the tightness of a line. Every fish demands an adjustment of the drag system depending on its size and strength, not too tight and not too loose.

One of the most common and unforgivable mistakes is having a drag set too tight. I lost countless fish, broke kilometers of line, and broke a good rod because of this simple mistake. Too much tightness doesn't allow real control over a fish but turns it into a bullfight in which the weakest link snaps in the blink of an eye.

This happened when I forgot to set the drag appropriately and when playing with drag unreasonably landing a fish. The outcome was always the same – standing disappointed and still believing that fish would jump on the bank with apologies.

Here, simple logic steps in. Nothing can withstand overwhelming pressure. Even metal breaks into pieces under enough stress. Engineers try to account for this and leave enough flexibility in the material.

Humans are the same. Overwhelming pressure in life and business result in stress that leaves cracks in minds

LOOSE OR TIGHT

and souls. We are all covered with these invisible scars within us. If the stress grows too much, we break.

Bad leaders of command-and-control style leadership set their drag systems too tight. They leave people with the cracks of stress all the time and lose them in the end, even the strongest ones.

Good leaders always allow margins for flexibility considering that humans are not made of steel and deserve such gaps of tolerance.

When under stress, we even tend to blame ourselves for not being strong enough to withstand pressure, forgetting that we all have limits. My mentor and friend, Marshall Goldsmith, father of executive coaching and #1 leadership thought leader in the world, always says, "You are only a human. Forgive yourself for being a human."

You have a meeting canceled at the last moment – enjoy this time. Your flight is delayed – get your cup o f coffee and relax thinking about something good. Have time for yourself. Don't be hooked by the things that will leave you cracked at the end. Such gaps or margins allow peace and resilience to carry on with your role and duties.

LESSONS LEARNED:

- Give yourself tolerance at the margins. As a leader, give your people even greater tolerance at the margins. We are only humans.

- There is no space for improvement and growth when you don't have flexibility. Nothing grows bigger than a box it is packed in. No one grows bigger in an environment of tight limits.

- Never deal with extremely busy people. They will end up cracked and will make you crack.

- Too much pressure and stress make people look for an exit.

- Loose or poor leadership encourages a lack of discipline, concentration, focus, and relevance. Such a leader leaves people disappointed.

"

*Too much pressure and stress
make people look for an exit.*

"

Passion to serve others is love expressed in quality action.

PASSION TO SERVE OTHERS

A few years ago, I was fly-fishing for salmon on one of those remote ice-cold arctic rivers, Kola, at the far end of Northern Europe. The season had just begun, and the largest fish were swimming in from the sea; aggressive, strong, and enormously beautiful. It was an early morning with a bit of frost covering everything, the first few proud fins breached the surface. I became focused, channeling my excitement through the fishing rod. Just a few casts and something big began tugging on the line. After a few seconds of fighting, this silver torpedo got under control...Bang! My favorite and well-tested Sage rod snapped. It is a traumatic experience for any fly fisherman – the fish is lost and a fisherman's best friend, his rod, is in pieces nearly ending the season when it has only just begun.

I promptly sent the rod to Sage for repairs. I even attached a note that I was in danger of losing the whole season. Within ten days I got my rod back fixed and good as new. I called the regional manager in the UK to thank him for the fantastic service, and for saving my season and praised him for the incredible rods they build. He appreciated my call and said, "We are all very passionate fly-fishermen, from the store clerk to our CEO. Passion for fishing and passion for our clients is what helps us build such outstanding rods and make people's experiences enjoyable. We know what you feel like losing the rod and did our best for you as a fellow fisherman."

Sincere passion and focused understanding of a customer's needs help businesses to enter the customer's own vision and become naturally accepted. Unity between a business's and customer's vision is the goal. Passion for customers and what they care about increases the business's understanding and care for them.

Passion added to customer care gets people, customers, and employees excited. Mutual excitement opens more potential and opportunity for both. Big ideas are built from and based on a shared passion.

Sympathy is not enough. Customers demand empathy. In our social lives, we take for granted that our friends and family walk with us. In commerce, a business needs first to cross the distance to the customers in order to walk with them. The business should never assume that the customer will cross that distance.

Customer champions love their customers first and often trust their instincts. They know numbers can't explain everything. Customers love them in return, mirroring the effort of a company in loyalty. I've heard business leaders say that they are lucky to have great customers. This has nothing to do with luck. The quality of customers reflects the effort spent in attracting them and how the organization sees them. If you passionately fight for them and love them, then your customers will be loyal, active, and happy to refer your products or services to their contacts. If one doesn't like customers, then he or she always sees them as greedy, nasty, and not responsive.

Being passionate about your team means asking questions almost daily – How do you feel? What worries you? What can I do for you? What plans do you have? The same questions should be asked in relation to customers. Unfortunately, even otherwise good organizations don't think of this.

LESSONS LEARNED:

- Passion to serve others is love expressed in quality action.

- We absorb and understand things that we listen to carefully, with a full heart. Listen to nature, and you will understand it. Listen to customers, and you will understand them. Listening is the most critical skill in business.

- Being naturally obsessed with customer care and satisfaction is a must. Customers are perceptive and will know when you are faking it.

- If all a business does is look for problems, that is what they will find. Look for solutions, and they will come.

- As a visionary coach, I have a simple approach – your success is my goal. Think big about success creating value for people, making positive changes for them, and improving the quality of their lives.

- Your passion should show in the details. The result is quality that appeals to many generations. This is true passion.

"

If all a business does is look for problems, that is what they will find. Look for solutions, and they will come.

"

When in doubt, don't be doubtful – stay on the course of your vision.

DOUBTS

On the bridge of a trawler on which I made several trips, there was a sign, "When in doubt, call the captain in."

With my little experience in those days, I asked the captain what this sign meant.

His explanation was simple and to the point. "We have three core aims – catch and process as much fish as possible, withstand the storms, and get back home safely. If you are doubtful about what to do, think of the aims and how what you do fulfills these. If you are still doubtful, ask me." This was a brilliant explanation – keep navigating against the waves, be productive in fishing, and think of people's safety as the main priority. When in doubt, ask for help or clarification.

Later, I realized that doubts are indicators of a lack of knowledge and data, and not knowing where to go and what to do. Doubts tear our minds apart if we do not know where we are going and our goals. They paralyze our productivity.

Doubts greatly undermine execution and waste energy and resources. You can easily spot someone in doubt by the way he or she bounces in all directions. It is like a mental poison making one powerless and blind to his or her own potential.

One of the core leader's roles is to be clear with a direction and communicate it to people restlessly. If a leader is not clear about his or her direction and aims, people blindly follow short-term instructions, burying their doubts until they grow to a point they can't be concealed. This leads to the organization's failure.

Doubts grow from a lack of clarity and block decision-making.

God gives us the gift of decision-making. The devil offers us a myriad of choices. Without a clear vision, a leader gets lost in those choices.

Vision begins with a firm decision to make a difference. Its success directly depends on the decisive and focused implementation of that decision. The ability to do so separates visionaries from wannabes.

Decision-making stands on enabling and purpose. Enabling reflects a leader's role in empowering people by providing clarity of purpose, standing for inspiring values, and enhancing decision-making capacity. Purpose allows people to navigate the challenges the market will inevitably present. Detours may need to be made along the way but vision keeps you moving in the right direction. Even complex decisions become simple if aligned with a vision and values.

Decisiveness is a property of a free people. One must be free to be able to make decisions and one must make decisions to remain free. What does this mean? A clear understanding of the goals gives freedom. Freedom is in knowing where to go and what is needed to make the journey. Simply recall the relief you felt when a decision was made. It was like a heavy burden taken off your shoulders. You felt free.

Enabled decision-making helps to navigate uncertainty to the desired destination. When people are free to know where to go and what they aim to achieve, they generate incredibly valuable ideas and make well-balanced decisions. They realize that their decision must generate solutions and value, not more problems, and direct their thoughts and actions accordingly. They grow and make the vision more compelling by adding more value to it. They are free from doubt.

No one said that decisions are easy, particularly at the strategic level, but it still is a skill that must be trained to the highest possible level. This skill is essential if you think about being a visionary leader.

LESSONS LEARNED:

- When in doubt, don't be doubtful – stay on the course of your vision.

- When in doubt – ask for expert help. This is only a sign of you aiming to be effective and needing more knowledge.

- If you are doubtful, then employees' reactions will be doubtful or even negative.

- Leadership is about challenging people's inner doubts and helping them out of their mental bubbles.

- Vision is the organization's North Star. A shared vision is a collective asset that makes them giants. People empowered to make decisions become giants who make execution possible regardless of the project's complexity.

- A leader without vision generates only doubt.

"

When in doubt – ask for expert help. This is only a sign of you aiming to be effective and needing more knowledge.

"

*Your vision must be greater
than your problems.*

TINY DEVILS

With the first small and gentle leaves appearing and the air warming up a bit, clouds of mosquitoes take control of the air. Regardless of the weather, in wind or rain, these tiny evils of the North are on the bloody hunt for every live creature in their way. Humans are their prime target.

Legions of these vampires are everywhere. They go into every tiny gap in the clothing, finding every bit of exposed flesh to sink their needles into.

You can't ignore mosquitoes. Once, I fell asleep by the campfire forgetting to spray mosquito repellent and woke up with bruises on my face looking like a boxer after a tough fight thanks to all the bites.

They can turn a person into a bundle of inflamed nerves. One of my in-laws, a big and strong guy, visited us and I took him for a two-day trip to show him nature and get him into fishing. In a matter of a few hours, he got an allergy shock and a fever, forcing us back home.

In the times of the Soviet Union, it was a torture-death in Gulag camps – putting someone naked on mosquitoes. It was known as *komariki* (mosquitoes). This is an incredibly brutal and slow torture to death.

It's impossible to fight every insect. You have to find a way to protect yourself so you can move on with the day. You can use a mosquito net or use mosquito repellents. Repellents are effective and don't restrict your movements as mosquito nets do. Also, there is a belief that some kind of antibody against mosquito bites tends to develop every season allowing one to be more tolerant of the bites and use less repellent.

In simple terms, if you can't find a solution against mosquitoes, you simply can't continue fishing and enjoy nature.

In terms of leadership, all businesses face a myriad of problems that, like mosquitoes, suck blood and energy from them. Having problems is normal unless they turn into deadly challenges.

In personal or business life, we mainly hear people talk about problems. Many people proudly declare on their social media profiles and CVs that they are "problem-solvers." However, talking about problems only causes more problems.

Great leaders talk about solutions. We have enough problem-solvers; we need more solution-finders. The main challenge for today's businesses is the lack of vision that reflects long-term solutions for others.

Without a strong vision for the future, many leaders are not in a position to fight against today's problems. They think about problems only and not about the future, lacking a strong and compelling vision and the ability to tap into the future with confidence. Of course, the future doesn't send an email to anyone with clear plans. It demands a clear vision.

To win in the marketplace, your vision and goals must be greater than your problems. Vision is a multidimensional space in the future that reflects the value offered for others.

The greatness of a vision matters more than the size of the organization. Great vision allows organizations to grow and remain valuable for many years to come.

Without vision, a leader turns into a problem-solver or a mosquito fighter who doesn't have much chance to focus on creating the future.

LESSONS LEARNED:

- Your vision must be greater than your problems.

- When your goals are greater than your problems, you change your mindset to achieve them. When you don't have great goals, your problems determine your way of thinking.

- Limited thinking defines limited goals. A strong mindset defines goals that go beyond the ordinary.

- Problem-solving doesn't make anyone successful. Success is defined by the solutions found and executed.

- If your mindset is attuned to finding problems, you will find many more of them. If your mindset is attuned to finding solutions, you will find many brilliant solutions.

"

Limited thinking defines limited goals. A strong mindset defines goals that go beyond the ordinary.

"

Simplicity is a virtue of reliability.

RELIABLE SIMPLICITY

Learning how to tie strong knots is a fishing basic. Mastery is in how to tie fewer knots. It took me a while to imprint this firmly into my fishing and leadership practice.

I began thinking about this after a good few of my first trips and losing fish for a seemingly strange reason.

Once, a decent, but not large salmon took my fly, and after a few minutes of resistance, the fish broke the line almost effortlessly. I reeled back the remaining line finding that it was snapped on or very near the knot. My first reaction was to blame the line. This was the easiest. I checked the line for strength pulling it with all my power – it held perfectly well. So, something was wrong with what I did.

Some experienced fishermen solved my problem.

My mistake was simple – every knot weakens the line. The nylon fishing line loses about 50% of its strength on every knot, and the modern fluorocarbon line weakens by about 15% on every knot. Tackle is torn at the knots.

Indigenous peoples of the Arctic manage to catch salmon with a tin can. Don't laugh. They simply wind the fishing line around the jar and tie a heavy lure. The lure is thrown by hand, and that empty jar serves as a reel. Everything is brilliantly simple. Three simple elements – fishing line, lure, tin can, and just one knot to tie the lure. Believe me or not – this works perfectly well.

Simplicity means reliability. Every knot makes my tackle weaker and more complicated and less effective.

Another similar mistake that I realized when I once again was taming a tangled fishing line, getting angrier by the moment. Solving puzzles because of my tendency to make things complicated wasn't my plan. I paid the price for complicating things again.

Simplicity is the religion of the fisherman. Make simplicity sophisticated. In fishing, every complication makes the distance between a fisherman and a caught fish greater.

Every element of my tackle must be reliable and serve its purpose. Every part must be excellent in its functionality. Every hook must be razor sharp, and lines straight without tangles and knots. In other words, a blind hook means an empty bag.

RELIABLE SIMPLICITY

In business, every complication makes execution difficult and the distance between a company and customers greater, thus questioning success in the marketplace.

Leadership demands disciplined simplicity.

A vision is not a vision unless it's understood. Simplicity lets people believe in the vision. If the vision is complicated most people will ignore it. Therefore, even a vision's physical form must be simple. Vision operates and makes execution possible from its simplicity.

The simpler the vision in its core meaning, the easier it can be shared with employees, customers, and partners, and thus it's easier to scale inside and outside an organization. The simplicity of a vision allows it to be shared easily with and between employees, from employees to customers, and among customers.

Complication is the enemy of great vision. If things are too complicated and too difficult to grasp, then most likely this is not a real vision but an overcomplicated puzzle. No one can solve complex problems for people without attracting supporters and developing empathy on a big scale if the vision is too complicated. Too much complexity simply turns people off.

Simple is always better, yet simple is often more difficult. We are often taught to make every process more complicated. We were never taught how to make things simple, which is necessary for leadership.

LESSONS LEARNED:

- Simplicity is a virtue of reliability.

- If people can't understand it easily, then they can't pursue it or achieve it. If you can explain it to a ten-year-old with a handful of words and they understand, then your vision is simple enough.

- Professionals tend to present complex ideas in simple words. Pretenders tend to use technical language to justify themselves, not ideas.

- Simplicity connects vision with people and makes vision achievable. Complication makes vision dysfunctional and unachievable.

- Simplicity makes people productive in achieving their goals. Complication makes people busy solving problems that are created by it. A true leader must be a master of simplicity.

"

Simplicity connects vision with people and makes vision achievable. Complication makes vision dysfunctional and unachievable.

"

Many are enthusiastic until it comes to responsibility and hard work.

SMALL OR LARGE

I remember my first salmon as my first love – ideal in its perfection, strong, shiny, silvery with a dark-purple-black back top of five kilos. She hid deep in front of a large underwater rock. I still can't explain what triggered her to take my lure.

For someone new wearing fishing waders for a couple of times only, this was a great success. Probably, the river gods credited me for something. Or I just got lucky.

Then, a few trips in a row, I had no fish at all. I prayed to the river spirits for any salmon. Actually, I was cheating – I prayed for any fish but dreamed about large, huge salmon.

One day, I got what I prayed for. A two-kilo salmon took my fly exactly at the moment the fly touched the surface. This small fish gave me a lot of trouble hassling up and down the pool and making all possible pirouettes, almost dancing "Swan Lake" prima solo.

My unsaid prayers and patience were finally rewarded, just much later. I caught my first ten-kilo salmon towards the end of the season.

The second season was much more successful with about twenty large salmon landed and a lot of small salmon, or grills as they are often called. It looked like the river spirits were testing and trying me in the first season.

With more experience, more knowledge, and greater first-hand data, I started noticing the difference between small and big salmon.

Small salmon or grills are enthusiastic and energized. They are always ready for a show with paparazzi snapping photos on the bank of the river. Grills jump fully out of the water, curious, and playful. They are always exploring shallows, gaps between underwater rocks, and gatekeeping deep pits.

Large mature fish are usually shy and show only the top fin or tail if breaking the surface. Large salmon love staying deep in front of big stones where the water is the deepest and always fresh. They patrol their pool at particular times of the day and can cover huge underwater distances in a split second remaining unnoticed.

Small salmon are easily tricked because of their curiosity and lack of experience. Grills eagerly grab a fly as a child grabs a bright new toy – "bang." To catch a grill, you need to be good at the traditional approach.

SMALL OR LARGE

Provoking a large salmon to take a fly is a totally different story. Large fish know everything and all the fishermen's tricks and have enough experience to write an encyclopedia. Catching mature fish demands a specific and delicate approach. Even the way large fish take a fly is very interesting. You may feel gentle touches to your fly a few times like a "tip-tip" that you may leave unnoticed. This is the way this smart fish tests your faith and patience. Then, it could be a gap in touches, and then, a strong long pull would happen. You will feel this difference in the tug power of this river monster. Stay firm on your feet – the fish caught you.

In simple words, small salmon are very enthusiastic whereas large salmon are calm and confident.

I was thinking about achieving success using the analogy of catching small and large salmon. A leader should understand the difference between small wins and serious successes. They are different in their nature and thus, demand different and unique approaches.

Small wins are very important on the journey to achieve something big. They are stepping stones on the ladder of success. Think about big wins while learning how to achieve small wins. They allow honing the mastery of doing things in traditional ways, or to play by the rules.

As it is impossible to catch only large salmon, it is impossible to have only big successes in life and in business. Be grateful for small wins. They feed your aspiration for serious success.

The big win resides deep and doesn't show itself much. Big success demands calm, confidence, and mastery in setting your own rules.

A small salmon could be caught because of its aggressive enthusiasm. Catching large salmon demands confidence, calmness, and mastery. Until you learn how to catch small fish, it is useless to try to catch big fish. Until you learn to manage yourself even in small things, it is useless to lead people to great success.

LESSONS LEARNED:

- Many are enthusiastic until it comes to responsibility and hard work.

- Enthusiasm is good when supported by unique knowledge and mature confidence. Enthusiasm supported by only social media likes is irresponsible.

- Small wins help the mind to grow ready for a big success. We cease to be mindful when neglecting small wins and stopping our minds from growing.

- As quality turns quantity into value, mastery in creating value for others turns one from a one-time winner into a leader of success.

- Commitment, competence, and confidence always beat unjustified enthusiasm.

"

A great partner is a blessing allowing you to go very far and withstand any challenges.

PRETENDING TO BE THE BROWN BEAR AND A GREAT PARTNERSHIP

The Arctic is the most difficult place to live. I have lived almost half of my life in the Arctic and still love it. It remains in my DNA. It brings out your true self.

It's a harsh environment where you can experience all four seasons in one day. When I brought my wife Zagidat, a woman from the warm south to the Arctic, she was shocked to see heavy snow falling horizontally on May 31st. I tell her, "Hurry up, take pictures, this is the last snow in May, and we will photograph the June snow in June."

This is a place where you fully realize – I am not the master of nature, I only have the privilege of being a part of it. The Arctic is the place where you have the greatest opportunity to see yourself as part of a vast, open system, not the master of nature, rather a small but important part of it.

The Arctic is a place where you must unconditionally help others and be grateful for every little help you receive. Here the risks are high and the consequences can be dramatic. The conversation is direct and if someone asks for help, they really need it. Here you value friendship most of all.

I have a great friend, Igor, with whom we went through many fishing adventures and faced many difficult situations. Once, we decided to go fishing for brown trout in the chain of lakes far away in the tundra and only about one kilometer away from the Barents Sea coast.

Besides fishing, we wanted to gather Arctic roots. Arctic root or Golden root (Rhodiola rosea) is similar to the well-known Ginseng. Arctic root helps to increase energy, stamina, strength, and mental capacity, improve athletic performance, resist the effects of stress, and help manage depression, anxiety, and other symptoms. Saami and Lapland people believe that Arctic root takes strength from the rocks and gives it to people. The root grows only about one centimeter per year so a thirty-centimeter root has been growing for thirty years.

It was late September and the first patches of snow were scattered everywhere along the tundra. The vegetation was nearly gone which made it difficult to spot the desired root. I decided to dig out a few roots that looked right to me. Then I ate them without blinking an eye. Something wasn't right and we

PRETENDING TO BE THE BROWN BEAR AND A GREAT PARTNERSHIP

decided to go for roots near the mouth of the creek after fishing.

In a couple of hours, I felt sick. Everything was blurry. I was rushing for a toilet again and again. It was a limbo between falling asleep and rushing outside. I lost about ten kilos of weight in one day.

We decided to get back home. Igor took my heavy backpack and went ahead of me, paving the way, making tea, and helping on steep ascents and descents. We walked for a few hours back to the car and by that time I got a bit better.

Here we met a local Saami guy who was chasing reindeer. He looked at me and asked what was wrong. I explained my experiment of testing different roots. The guy laughed for minutes and then explained, "Before going for a few months to a den for a winter sleep, the brown bear eats the root which helps to clean the digestive system. You are a brown bear with a clean stomach now. You ate this root." Now, at least, I know that transformation from a human to a brown bear is such fun.

An old African proverb says. "If you want to go quickly, go alone. If you want to go far, go together." This is so true in such circumstances. I'm grateful to Igor for his friendship and help. Thank you, partner!

LESSONS LEARNED:

- A great partner is a blessing allowing you to go very far and withstand any challenges.

- Being at the top is lonely. Have a partner who will help share the journey.

- Friendship or partnership is about giving to gain. If you are not prepared to give first, you are not a leader.

- No one can clap with one hand. A partnership is clapping together with four hands. Make your team partners in challenges and successes.

- Business is the toughest terrain in which no one can survive and succeed on their own.

- You don't need to be rich or to have a lot of resources to be a good partner. You need to be committed and willing to help.

"

*Friendship or partnership is about giving to gain.
If you are not prepared to give first, you are not a leader.*

"

Stagnation in explorative thinking leads to leadership short-sightedness.

KEEP EXPLORING

Successful fishermen explore as many pools and as many rivers as possible. Behind every bend and turn of the river, there is something incredible, something that allows you to see and learn something new and incredible. And to catch more fish, of course. Wonders happen when explored and will remain with you forever.

I'm grateful to my old friends and fishing companions who infused me with the craving to explore. Every fishing season, I walk along the rivers letting my mind wander and open it wider with every discovery. Even though I had no fish and was completely physically drained, I was excited to learn something new and be full of inner energy to explore more. Every step counts. Every little discovery enriches.

By exploring the rivers, I found that even with salmon being in almost every pool, there is an ultimate difference between the pools in terms of fishing. There are two types of pools – "transit" and "taking" pools. Salmon use "transit" pools for resting and grabbing a fly occasionally. They may look great but aren't very productive. "Taking" pools is what I'm looking for. Fish settle in such pools, inhabiting them, defending them, and attacking a fly revealing all its predator's reflexes.

Exploring gives you a better understanding of the hidden natural processes. Once, in the company of four old friends, we went fishing at the tidal part of Zapadnaya Litza that falls into the long and deep fjord of the Barents Sea.

It was full of fish! We never saw so many fish jumping out of the water in one day! We waded into the water and started our hunt. Salmon continued jumping everywhere, even at our feet, yet ignored everything and rocketed up upstream at the speed of a racing bolide.

We stopped fishing and decided to walk to the estuary aiming to find what was going on. The cause of that puzzle was somewhere there.

After twenty minutes of brisk walking, we noticed a large group of divers in black diving suits. We came closer and laughed at ourselves. They were seals popping up with a snort that we took for divers.

Aha! Seals are enemies of salmon. A seal eats about 25 kilos of salmon a day, and salmon are smart enough to find ways to escape being the seals' lunch, and they raced upstream.

All looked logical except we never saw so many seals in this fjord, and so close to the mouth of the river.

We went further along the fjord shore still curious to find the root cause. Here we found the answer to this mystery. We counted twelve shiny-black high fins cutting the surface of the fjord towards the river mouth. This was a band of orcas, the gangsters of the ocean. Orcas are not interested in salmon, they tried to block the seals into the end of the fjord for a feast. The seals then escaped into the shallows of the river mouth and used this as an opportunity to hunt salmon.

It looked like a battle scene with killer whales advancing on seals, which lined up running into shallow water and chasing salmon at the same time, and salmon, distraught with fear and hiding up the river where the seals could not climb because of the rapids.

It was impossible to see this battle from the river. We had to walk down the fjord to witness this once-in-a-lifetime experience. I never saw anything like this, even in the best documentaries. We learned more about nature and gained one more hint into the behavior of salmon.

One of the core differences between successful and ordinary fishermen is in exploring and knowing more about the river. Ordinary fishermen fish only at well-known pools. This may sound strange but it happens more commonly than could be assumed. Many people tend to imprison their freedom of exploring and nourishing their curiosity by thinking, "I wouldn't go there as I don't know what is there." Saying "no" to something breathtaking is voluntarily making life less meaningful. Keeping curiosity on a short leash is too expensive to miss.

We remain young as long as we have this "WOW" in our minds and hearts. Our ability to be surprised defines our real age. Keep exploring your river.

A Chinese proverb says, "A journey of a thousand miles begins with a single step." Take this step. Success waits to be discovered and explored. Success is on the other side of the discovery.

I learned one simple rule for personal and professional improvement – learn like a child when starting every new project or facing a new stage of life. Every exploration is full of "WOW" moments.

Leadership is about creating a vision for the future. A vision sees the abundance of the world within us and around us. Release your curiosity and passion for exploring, making yourself a better leader.

LESSONS LEARNED:

- Leadership is in action and exploring new opportunities, not in being today where you have been stuck yesterday and the day before.

- Stagnation in explorative thinking leads to leadership short-sightedness.

- A leader is a pathfinder into the future that he or she discovers first, and leads people to explore and enjoy it. A true leader is always on an explorative journey.

- Innovation is the result of curious minds boldly exploring possibilities and coming up with creative solutions. Nothing creative comes with the mindset that sticks with only well-known things.

- Learning allows one to explore something new, see new perspectives every time, and find how to get them working for people. What a leader brings to the table tomorrow comes from what has been explored and learned yesterday and today. If nothing new has been learned, then there is nothing new to be offered.

ENHANCING
LEADERSHIP

"

*I am always doing things I can't do –
that's how I get to do them.*

Pablo Picasso

> *Fishing is a lab of thinking while in nature. Leadership is a lab of thinking in which the future is created and where dogmas are questioned daily.*

THE MOST POWERFUL TACKLE

Atlantic salmon behave differently every season. Successful tactics from the previous season might not work this season. They like to keep you guessing.

One mid-summer season a few years ago we all faced a riddle. The salmon were hardly biting for an entire month. Something was wrong, not with the fish, but in the way we read their behavior.

I tried all the most reliable flies – Sunray Shadow, Collie Dog, Stoat's Tail, Ally's Shrimp, Francis, and many other flies. Nothing worked. It looked like laundering a fishing line and not fishing.

I did everything as prescribed – mornings, middays, midnights, evenings, right presentation, right flies, casting downstream as salmon prefers. Salmon kept jumping showing their silvery scale and sarcastically ignoring me. My confidence was next to nothing.

I had to change something. But what?

Nature gave me a hint. I noticed a nice fish that lay where I had no chance of using a traditional downstream cast. Here I decided to do something against the rules. Salmon is traditionally caught using a downstream cast. Trout prefers upstream casts. Why not treat salmon as trout?

A couple of relaxed casts and this silver torpedo eagerly took a fly. That was a fight! From this moment I was catching fish after fish, making that season one of my most successful.

This led me to think that even conservatively old and proven approaches must be questioned. It was nothing wrong with my tackle, it was a problem with my thinking. I used my mindset as a secondary function. As Aristotle said, "Be a free thinker and don't accept everything you hear as truth. Be critical and evaluate what you believe in." I took everything for granted before and was wrong.

I thought about our ancestors who lived hundreds of years ago in this hostile, cold environment. Ancestors were catching this smart fish without advanced modern tackle and succeeded. They didn't have graphite rods, space-aluminum reels, or strong fluorocarbon lines. Their mindset was their main tackle.

THE MOST POWERFUL TACKLE

Our remote ancestors were superhumans who survived in the hostile environment of the Arctic having almost nothing and finding peace with nature by expanding their mindset all the time.

An expanded mindset proves that we have unlimited opportunities. What you have at hand is important, yet what you have in your head makes the ultimate difference in the outcome. Even an ability to use tackle differently is defined by an ability to think differently. Make the most of your mindset as it is unlimited in capacity.

Mindset grows when faced with discomfort. Being comfortable when fishing in the Arctic is an oxymoron. If you expect comfort and ease you better stay home. It is the same in business – business is about challenging your comfort zone. Fishing and leadership are about being comfortable with being uncomfortable.

If something hadn't been done before, it doesn't mean it is wrong or you can't experiment. Be an entrepreneurial CEO. Mindset is your main tackle.

LESSONS LEARNED:

- Fishing is a lab of thinking while in nature. Leadership is a lab of thinking in which the future is created and where dogmas are questioned daily.

- Thinking differently expands your mindset. Mindset, not status, defines a leader's capacity. The resourcefulness of a leader is in a flexible mindset.

- We are given an expandable mindset to do more and achieve more. Use it for this purpose, don't limit it to the functionality of your leadership tools at hand.

- Flexible thinking is the mother of innovation and the father of the best solutions.

- Playing by the old rules is an excuse for those who don't want to use their main leadership tool – mindset.

- Rational thinking and clear execution must be stronger than emotions.

"

Thinking differently expands your mindset. Mindset, not status, defines a leader's capacity. The resourcefulness of a leader is in a flexible mindset.

"

No one can create a positive future with negative thoughts.

POSITIVITY FOR SUCCESS

I went fishing for salmon on one of the best days in the season. Everything looked very promising. Fish jumped out of the water waving with fins and tails. The weather was perfect – overcast with a slight breeze. Lucky me!

Yet, I had a conflict in the office on the previous day which occupied my mind and made me negative. Preparing for a trip, getting on a river, and casting was more mechanistic than natural because my thoughts were negative and far away.

I kept casting for hours without any luck. The fish ignored my fly even though it was presented straight t o their nose. Actually, this happened not once to me, but several times. I became tense and behaved like a jerk – lost a few flies and snapped the fly line. The fishing trip was ruined.

Somehow, nature and fish feel what mood you are in. Your mood literally affects you're fishing. If I'm positive – the fish is on a hook. If I'm negative – the fish ignore me. This is still a mystery to me how those creatures feel humans' moods.

I must be positive to interact with nature. I must be positive to be productive. I must be positive if I want to have energy within me.

Over the years, I've thought much about this experience. In my executive coaching practice, I have a simple rule – never coach uncoachable people. What defines whether a person is coachable or not?

First – Negative people are not coachable. They are toxic. Negativity does not allow us to look beyond ourselves and our own prejudices. It fuels doubt and unnecessary worries. Negative people will find a problem in every decision. Negativity does not allow us to look into the future. Negativity occupies every cell of your mind and blocks your path to success.

Second – Ungrateful people are never satisfied and never happy. They are looking for problems in everything and are very successful in creating more problems. I must be grateful for the opportunity to do what I love and for having what I have.

Third – Poor, know-it-all guys defend their ground at the cost of growth. They feel insecure about facing something unknown and pretend that they know everything.

Fourth – Ego-centric executives kill vision and blind us from seeing others and the world around us. The ego is the harshest master that is never satisfied while giving nothing in return.

I'm thankful to nature for this coaching lesson in leadership.

LESSONS LEARNED:

- Always smile and be grateful for every lesson, even negative ones. Smile, and people and the world will smile back at you.

- No one can create a positive future with negative thoughts.

- Your negativity is the highest barrier no one would be interested to overcome.

- Stay positive regardless of circumstances and don't let anyone infect you with their negativity.

- Negativity is the worst advisor. It always aims to make you feel like a victim of circumstances. It leads you to mistakes that you will regret greatly afterward.

> Strategy relies on humility accepting mistakes and learning from them.

GAME OF STRATEGISTS

A beautiful female salmon came to one of my favorite pools at a small remote river, and immediately took it under her rule. She showed up on the catwalk like a celebrity model, accompanied by a group of young male grills emphasizing her superiority.

This queen of the northern rivers was in the river a few times in her life and knew well how to stay unapproachably approachable. She showed up at different spots of the pool and hid away if even slightly disturbed.

She simply scoffed at me. After a couple of weeks without success, I made landing her a personal challenge. The gauntlet had been thrown.

With time, the fish moved behind the back side of the large underwater rock on the opposite side of the pool where she was unreachable.

I crossed the river at the shallow rapids below the pool, walked upstream, and took a position right above where the fish settled whilst keeping a low profile. I started casting a small "Stoat's tail" fly that looks very natural and started with short casts gradually decreasing the distance to this clever fish. The idea was simple – let her think that this fly is as natural as possible. In about eight or ten casts, the long-anticipated attack happened. She never saw a fly at this spot and took it eagerly. I landed this 12-kilo beauty after a good fight.

It wasn't just fishing. It was a contest between strategists in which position was key and how to approach the fish was critical.

Today, there are thousands of books on strategies available. Military academies and business schools use strategy cases from the old days. However, in the old days, kings and noblemen learned about warfare strategies through hunting. Their best military strategies were adopted from nature, and by the time they took the throne, they were well prepared. They learned strategy from nature.

Looking at my fishing journey, I realized the evolution of my thinking and attitude from an almost useless novice to a pirate that grabs easy trophies and to a strategist and then to a visionary. Nature transformed my mindset.

I must have a vision for every fishing trip and a strategy for how to approach the fish. Tactics depend on the situation. Playing tactics wouldn't get me many salmon; I needed strategy.

In his famous book, "The Art of War," an ancient Chinese philosopher and military genius, Sun Tzu noted, "All men can see the tactics whereby I conquer, but what none can see is the strategy out of which victory is evolved."

Fishing for such a smart fish as salmon, I must be strategic – in preparation, in choosing a pool, in casting, and most importantly, in thinking. Strategy is the art of making good assumptions and defining the most efficient path to what I want to achieve. My strategy must be unique because salmon are quick at recognizing patterned approaches. This is the essence of every strategy – uniqueness.

Fishing begins at home, in winter when preparing for a season. The key point is what I wouldn't do. This is about using fewer resources in the most effective way to achieve more.

With the beginning of a season, the data collection begins. I collect data by listening to others about what happened in the river over the last few days. This is about foreseeing and predicting the behavior of fish and not about doing something that worked before. I must be very careful in evaluating the battlefields and knowing about them as much as possible – water level, temperature, the color of the water, weather, tides, and many other things. Simply put, I need data about how the fish feels now and what could change.

I must be smooth like a fish in the water approaching a fish and strategic with my casts presenting a fly. I must step back to see the whole picture – the environment of fish, underwater conditions, a particular part of a season's behavior, and the usual preferences of fish at that given time. These will define where and how I will cast my fly – at shallows or at deeps, at the edge of the water or at the middle of a stream, by my feet or at a distance.

Little thought, nothing caught is my mantra. Salmon fishing is a game of strategists and success depends on the strategic choices I have made.

In leadership, strategy is about gaining an advantage in the marketplace. In fishing, strategy is about winning in the river against nature. Therefore, I must think big.

LESSONS LEARNED:

- Tactics are played as a priority when a strategy is not clear.

- Success in the market depends on your strategy.

- Strategy relies on humility accepting mistakes and learning from them.

- Be strategically savvy as you can apply it to everything you do.

- Leadership is a game that requires you naturally to think in strategic terms.

- Becoming a visionary who foresees and controls market spaces is always a winning strategy.

"

The responsibility of a leader is a mark of high quality of thoughts, actions, and outcomes. This is what people must notice first and foremost.

AN OBSERVED OBSERVER

Season after season, I was fishing at one of the least visited pools on my favorite river, Ura in the Kola Peninsula. It is an 'L' shaped deep pool with a long shallow stretch at the tail of it, a sandy bank on one side, and a few tall standing rocks on the opposite bank.

Here, I had a very peculiar "friend," a seagull with a yellowish spot on its neck. Almost every time I was on the river, she flew in with a squeaky noise, sat on the rock, and observed me for a while. The seagull didn't make a mess as seagulls usually do and was philosophically quiet observing me. It wasn't just another seagull, it was my companion, and I gave her a name – Marta.

Every time, after Marta took her post, I had a fish in an hour or less. I gutted and cleaned the fish and threw the guts and gills to Marta. She swiftly grabbed and greedily swallowed this lunch, and flew away with the same squeaky noise. It looked as if Marta was confident about me catching a fish and having her share of the catch. Otherwise, what was the point of her waiting around?

It was absolutely logical that Marta spotted fish coming into the river with the tide. In fact, Marta's visit was a signal for me that fresh salmon had entered the pool and I had a good chance to hook a few. Marta helped me as an unmanned guiding drone seeing something I couldn't.

Either the seagull was watching me, or I was watching the seagull. The situation was absolutely comical, yet, it was something to learn a lesson from.

Nature has many eyes even if you don't see them watching you while you're trying to observe. This man-seagull mutual observation and collaboration led me to think about how this works in leadership.

Many eyes are watching a leader at every moment. The higher the level of the leader, the more eyes are on him or her – hundreds, even thousands. Employees, customers, competitors, and society all observe a leader. At the same time, a leader observes people to the extent he or she is capable.

On one hand, leadership assumes responsibility, immediate and extended. The greater the vision of a leader then the greater the responsibility for its impact on people's lives, and the legacy that will be left afterward.

The reason is simple – every business success begins with responsibility. The same applies in our personal life where responsibility for others is taken for granted. No great achievement is ever built on blaming others, but rather on taking responsibility for others. Leadership is like being on Broadway 24 hours a day, 365 days a year, with a spotlight on everything you do.

The degree of responsibility depends on the magnitude of the leadership's vision. Thus, your every action is observed in detail.

On the other hand, while aiming to be in control of the market, a leader is carefully observed by customers who define that market. Market players are on alert for your every move anticipating gaining something from you.

A leader is never left alone and remains like a celebrity under paparazzi lenses. The leader is always an observed observer who does not always realize his or her weak point. Employees and customers have the best vantage point of seeing that. Leaders realize this and listen accordingly.

LESSONS LEARNED:

- People are in a superior position as observers of a leader as they see everything he or she does, good or bad.

- If you notice that people are not watching you, then this is a signal that they are not interested in your leadership anymore and are looking at someone else. You lost.

- How do you understand your responsibility?

- What you try not to show is getting observed most.

- The responsibility of a leader is a high quality of thoughts, actions, and outcomes. This is what people notice first and foremost.

"

*What you try not to show
is getting observed most.*

"

*Leadership is about being firm
in creating true value,
not about being nice.*

PICKY FISH

I always aim to catch a large fish, as any fisherman does. You never heard about a fisherman dreaming about catching a small fish.

Yet, I have no idea what fish will take my fly, small or large. Most often, just catching one fish makes my day. Why, when there are so many salmon in the river, fish don't take that juicy, well-proven, and so attractive fly?

Yes, we know that salmon don't feed in a river, and are picky about flies, and no one knows what is on its mind. Blah-blah-blah...The same answers again and again. I'm too curious and still want to understand what is going on there, under the surface.

There are countless times when I faced a situation when salmon ignored everything. I had gone through the shaman menu list preaching, dancing, and spitting over the shoulder with no response. This is ridiculous. I can sense fish and even see them here and there. Yet, they refuse to take the fly.

On one of my fishing trips to Iceland, we had an "okay" day with a couple of fish in the fridge. I chatted with the guide who knew much more about salmon than I did. The discussion turned to a salmon that just wouldn't respond. Here the guide looked at me and philosophically stated, "Oleg, this is a global issue."

"I will show you something." He pulled out his iPad and started a video. It was underwater footage of salmon at the river we fished and at exactly the pool familiar to me.

With a camera going down in the water, my jaw dropped wider. With no sign of fish at the surface, there were about twenty-five salmon camouflaging tightly laying together at the boom of the pool in one place – from small two-three-kilo grills to trophy-sized mature ones. Then, someone cast a fly which was clearly seen on the screen. The fish didn't respond a few times. Then, a small grill moved out of the school and scouted the fly without touching it. The same happened a couple more times. Then, on the next cast, a different fish suddenly attacked the fly and was caught. Only 4% of fish responded to the fly.

Meanwhile, the whole school of fish didn't show even the slightest signs of disruption. They continued meditating.

I was speechless. I was totally wrong assuming that there were only a few fish in the pool. In fact, it was full of fish, they just didn't care about the fly. They were simply not interested. Fish are not picky. This is us having little understanding of its life. This is the natural order that must be accepted.

This underwater footage didn't give me an answer to why a fish doesn't take a fly but gave me a hint that it is possible to have a response from a few of them.

This was a great insight that led me to think about different things relevant to fishing, and to business and leadership as well. My thoughts bounced back to leadership, marketing, influence, and support.

When we offer a product to the market, we assume that it will be of an interest to the majority of customers. In fact, only a tiny percentage of people respond to our offer.

Support is of great importance in leadership. At the same time, having a team together is a critical task, and in most cases, engagement is not sufficiently high. Being a leader, you already know that not everyone understands you and not everyone is even willing to understand you.

You are a leader because you can encourage people to work together and respond to your call for action. Yes, this is not easy. Leadership is not about gaining social media likes which are fairly meaningless. This is about being firm when you lead people and they will respond to your confidence.

You must offer people a vision that is greater than they are, and greater than the organization, and make them the co-owners of the vision showing them how to contribute and what they will gain for themselves. You will have the highest response from people you can imagine.

LESSONS LEARNED:

- The beginning of the leadership journey is not easy. Don't expect everyone to support you. Count on those who stand by your side. You must create supporters starting from this point.

- Leadership is about being firm in creating true value, not about being nice. Value is what all people are quick to respond to. People always respond to something with greater meaning in their lives.

- Your market is much greater than you assume. The only matter is to offer something that will make people wake up and jump.

- We are still biological creatures and the natural order is still relevant to us.

- There is always something that holds people back from responding. People are not picky. We simply don't know enough about people.

"

We are still biological creatures
and the natural order
is still relevant to us.

"

*Involvement starts now.
Not next time, not next month,
right now.*

ACCIDENTAL EXPERIMENT ON COGNITIVE DISTANCE

Together with my old fishing companion, Igor we went fishing at a very interesting spot on the Kola River. We fished a couple of pools and came to a very promising spot with a bridge crossing the river. Surely, there must be salmon there hiding in the shadow of the bridge.

I started casting while Igor decided to cross the bridge to try his luck from the opposite bank. Somewhere in the middle of the bridge, Igor stood still and gazed into the water. He spotted a nice fish and my fly flowing around. "Hey, the fish doesn't react to your fly. Try again a bit closer to it." I cast again. "You almost hit her in the head and she moved away."

This was something I was very keen to watch myself. We quickly swapped positions – I went on the bridge and Igor took my spot and cast.

I never saw what happens in the water from such a perspective. When casting, I see everything from my perspective with a vague understanding of how casts are precise or appealing to the fish. Here, I had a chance to see what goes on almost from the fish's point of view.

This was incredibly interesting. The fish ignored the fly when it was about one meter or more away from her nose. The fly coming into her head from the side spooked the fish. When the fly was at a distance of that fish's length, a split-second attack happened, and Igor hooked the fish.

Ah-ha! Salmon reacts to a fly that is at the appropriate distance. For fish, this one meter is a distance that she sees as not deserving her effort whereas for a human the same distance of one meter is within the reach of a hand. If it is too close, a fish sees it as a threat. Therefore, salmon's preparedness to react is very similar to what we call cognitive distance.

I didn't understand this difference as I was viewing things from a fisherman's perspective only. Changing viewpoints made me think about how we consider effective cognitive distance in leadership.

We are creatures of nature and our reptile brain is selective in identifying what is threatening or important or could be ignored. Yet, our mindset commands the brain. If our default reflexes are in command, we remain primitive. If our mindset is bounded for growth and creating value for others is in command, it sets the brain to get closer to people and hear what they say at a wider range of cognitive distance.

Thus, our ability to understand and be understood, and communicate effectively greatly depends on the cognitive distance between a leader and his or her people.

A strong leader has the ability to grasp an ever-changing world. To be able to scale his or her vision one should maintain an appropriate cognitive distance from it. This allows us to see the broader picture while keeping the important details in sight. Standing too close only allows one to see the details while losing the whole picture. Standing too far away means losing important details from which the vision is created. In the first case, one loses the whole meaning of the vision for nothing. In the second case, the vision becomes detached from reality

In simple terms, cognitive distance defines our willingness and preparedness to listen with full attention and react appropriately.

How to maintain effective cognitive distance? The level of a leader's involvement greatly defines the effectiveness of cognitive distance. Of course, this is not the only, but still one of the most important factors which must be considered first.

Involvement begins with engaging interaction. A few minutes of genuine interaction are worth years of formal communication. Make every minute worth a year.

This is similar to a friendship in which a strong understanding of each other comes into play. Being connected and involved means partnering with employees on a full range of issues that have an impact on human life. This kind of care can affect personal and professional growth.

Building rapport and understanding demands daily involvement. To feel and understand people one should always have a place for them in his own mind and heart. Inconsistency undermines relations and makes the distance between a leader and people too great to react appropriately.

LESSONS LEARNED:

- People define optimal cognitive distance. This is for a leader to find it through daily involvement. Look at it from your people's viewpoint.

- Something that is not understood is never executed.

- Involvement starts now. Not next time, not next month, right now.

- No one would believe in a "Santa Claus-style" leader who they see once a year, especially one likely to be bearing bad news.

- A leader that defends his or her own status remains ignored and not heard. Take your crown off and be close to people.

"

A piece-of-mind solution comes out of peace of mind.

PEACE

One of the most praised things in human life is peace. One of the least exercised things in our life is peace. Strangely or not, we tend to neglect or overlook something critically important to us, whether in our personal life or business. We hardly have time to find peace, even at the cost of doing something meaningless.

We are living in a world in which things are praised for being loud and attention-getting, regardless of substance. Such things prevent us from having a better sense of the world around us.

We need peace to be at peace with nature and ourselves.

On a very bright day, which salmon don't like at all, I cast and cast for a few hours. The water was too clear, there were no shadows; the fish felt very uncomfortable and insecure in such conditions. There was no point in continuing.

I gave up and sat to relax and enjoy the beautiful nature. Somehow, I was immersed in the tranquility of the universe and was at peace. It was some kind of meditation, which I'm normally not good at. Yet, I found myself at total peace with myself and with the environment. This was so powerful and mind-opening.

I hardly noticed the time. Whether it took fifteen minutes or an hour, I can't say, and I came out with a clear feeling about what to do next. On the second cast of a tiny blue-silver-colored fly, a four-kilo sea trout that only came into the river from the sea firmly took my offering. It was a terrific fight. This splendid fish jumped fourteen times out of the water and showed herself like a celebrity on the red carpet.

I realized that when I'm at peace with nature and myself, it rewards me. When I love my people, when I'm at peace with them, I am rewarded as a leader by their engagement and loyalty. Any tension with nature makes us distant from the world. Friction and tension ruin the connectedness of minds and hearts and make leadership meaningless.

I remember the start of this path of visionary leadership as if it happened yesterday. On one fishing trip, I climbed to the top of a mountain in the middle of nowhere. I sat at the top and gazed around into this great tranquil wilderness, basking in the solitude.

Suddenly I realized how little, powerless, inconsequential, imperceptible, and insignificant I am compared to this world. Something whispered within me, "What is the meaning of what I do? What do I do for the future? Who am I and where do I want to be? How can I escape mediocrity?"

This was a moment of peace in which I envisioned my book *The Vision Code: How to Create and Execute a Compelling Vision for Your Business* in detail, breaking the code of vision and turning it into a simple practical algorithm for the first time.

Peace gifts us with the ability to think big. Being in nature is the best opportunity to find peace and become better, stronger, and with a clear mind.

LESSONS LEARNED:

- Peace makes us pure. It gives clarity to thoughts and actions. Fifteen minutes in peace is more productive than days of brainstorming under pressure.

- When in peace, you can explore a huge world within you that you can travel endlessly.

- A piece-of-mind solution comes out of peace of mind.

- When people see a leader being not at peace, they leave.

- Peace makes you positive. Positive thoughts allow the creation of a positive future. This is important as no one can create a positive future with negative thoughts.

"

*The voice of intuition
can either warn us off
or encourage us on.*

INTUITION

I strongly believe in intuition, and every interaction with nature makes me believe in intuition even more. Here I must admit that I'm not an expert in psychology and my observations are less scientific and more from life experience.

Intuition guards me against wrong action or inaction and directs me somewhere unthinkable for my good. This is like an Angel silently whispering in my mind, "Don't do this" preventing me from overconfidence and assumptions or, "Do this as it is the best solution for you even when not visible and seemingly beyond your capacity."

Every time I've ignored my gut, I've paid for it. I went fishing after a week-long pouring rain that overflowed all the local rivers. What could go wrong on a small, well-explored river where I knew almost every pool and stone? I decided to cross the river which I did many times before. Something in my mind said, "Don't do this. Stay where you are." I was overconfident and promptly waded into the water. Just a few meters away from the opposite bank, I fell into an underwater pit that wasn't there before.

Where it was normally about waist-deep, the water was above my head. I swam to that opposite bank snorting like a seal and thinking about how to return back without much adventure. I cursed myself for not listening to my intuition.

Following my intuition always leads to good outcomes, even beyond good. I packed for a two-day fishing trip on one of the remote rivers of the Kola Peninsula in the last days of August. The weather forecast was promising and I was ready to leave in a couple of hours. However, I was taking my time as something protested within me. Then, I got a phone call and realized something else I had to do. The strength and frequency of this gut feeling kept increasing, and I gave up the idea and went for a few hours fishing on the river in less than a two-hour drive.

Later, one of my friends called me with very interesting news. The old wooden bridge on the road I was intending to take was washed away by the rain, leaving a few people stranded on the far side of the bridge. Lucky me! Thanks to my gut!

As an Indian philosopher and researcher of the nature of the mind, Jiddu Krishnamurti wisely noted, "Intuition is the whisper of the soul."

We are only humans and our minds are full of illusions. Illusion is like a morning mist that comes from nowhere and disappears with the first bright rays of sunshine. It comes without hard thinking and disappears with the first clear thoughts about what underlies it. The reason is simple – the illusion is not attached to reality and only tricks the mind.

Intuition or instinct is something very different than an illusion. It is rooted in our perception of the world and attaches our souls and unconscious minds to the universe. This is something that is very difficult to explain but extremely powerful if well-developed. A gut feeling is very real and helps us to make the right choice even in very unclear situations.

Intuition mobilizes a superior inner consciousness that processes weak signals and connects seemingly unconnected dots that the brain, eyes, ears, and other sensing centers absorb without us noticing. It is our best inner compass.

In leadership, intuition is as vitally important as in fishing. This almost animal perception is a critical element on which ideas are often built initially, and no profound vision can be created without it. This gut feeling helps to make decisions in complex contexts when limited data is available or when we feel an inconsistency in that data. In some sense, our mind and soul do optimization in a much finer way than our logical brain does. Even such a genius as Albert Einstein stated, "The intuitive mind is a sacred gift and the rational mind is a faithful servant."

Our understanding of tomorrow is superficial to a great extent and can't be fully grasped by simple logic. It lies beyond the convenient logic of today. A visionary leader fully realizes this fact and listens to his gut. The future talks to those who are prepared to listen and rewards them with great vision.

Young leaders often ask me how to develop intuition. I don't have the exact recipe but there are a few things that I've noticed.

Intuition builds on experience and on an ability to analyze and process details and asking counterintuitive questions and being prepared to accept inconvenient answers. Be prepared to listen more and be in silence more. Rumi said, "Why are you so afraid of silence? Silence is the root of everything."

INTUITION

Let your intuition speak and be prepared to act on its guidance.

LESSONS LEARNED:

- The voice of intuition can either warn us off or encourage us on.

- Intuition becomes stronger when you listen to it. Intuition stops sending signals when you stop listening to it.

- We need intuition to see certainty through the mist of uncertainty.

- The highest human inner feelings such as love, kindness, and intuition are superior gifts from nature. Don't try to rationalize them if you don't want to lose them.

"

*Listening precedes learning.
It allows us to think more, feel
and gain more, and give others
what is needed.*

CALL FOR PURITY

Ice fishing in the Arctic is something special – challenging and exciting. Imagine yourself in the middle of a calm, snow-white land of rocks and water covered with thick ice. You are fifty kilometers from the nearest human habitat and, thank God, civilization has not reached this place. You feel like a primitive man of the ice age. There is no one and nothing around except birds, arctic foxes, wolverines, and deer. The silence is absolute, sometimes interrupted by the whistle of the wind. This is the dream of every person tired of the noise of office life.

Together with my friend, Andre, I went ice fishing at one such place. We left our car in the village on the edge of the tundra, and drove further by snowmobile. Wo-hoo! Three days of pure joy! Nothing can be better for fishing fanatics.

We promptly put up a tent, threw reindeer skins on a tent floor, prepared sleeping bags, and drilled holes in meter-thick ice. No force can stop a man with a rod who senses a fish.

The first day brought us a lot of arctic char and brown trout. Thanks to the gods of the tundra! Actually, on the first day, you only get connected with nature and overexcited catching strong and smart fish.

On the second day, from early morning we went into different spots on this huge lake, and away from our tent. It was calmer, easier to connect with nature. When you feel connected, you start immersing in the wilderness envisioning a mammoth walking out from behind a rocky hill and feeling ready to fight a bear. No wonder ancient Greeks named arctic l ands Hyperborea, the land of mythical superhumans. This land can be described in two words – purity and strength.

Suddenly, I heard my mobile phone ringing. I jumped up and looked around. The signal was strong, but this was impossible for a simple reason – I left my phone in the car, fifty kilometers away. Here, I realized to what extent my brain is polluted with noises, not allowing me to think deeply. Non-stop calls, gadgets, TV, social media, and a million other noises. The excessive noise blocked me from listening to people and the environment. It made me dumb.

This reminded me of an old story when a chatty woman asked a priest, "Why God doesn't talk to me?" And the priest responded, "How can God talk to you when you talk all the time? You can't hear him responding."

Noise that we allow to penetrate our mind turns me from being an authentic human into an artificial human being where nature teaches us to stand still and listen to the environment and ourselves. That was a shockingly powerful discovery.

I talked with Andre over this in the evening and agreed not to talk the next day. No words unless necessary. A miracle happened. I started hearing even the slightest noises – partridges tweeting far away, birds swishing in the sky, an arctic fox staring at me from afar, and many other phenomenal things around me.

This mysterious call was needed for me to understand how much I was losing. I learned to listen and understand. I realized that in leading my team I was mainly responding, not listening to understand. I wasn't an involved leader; I was a talking head responding to every noise, not hearing what had been said and what people felt.

LESSONS LEARNED:

- Listening connects minds and hearts.

- Keep your mind pure. Purity of mind defines your leadership capacity.

- Listening precedes learning. It allows us to think more, feel and gain more, and give others what is needed.

- Being overly busy means being less productive and losing the ability to think deeply and act appropriately. Never be busy for important things. It will cost you quality of life and the enjoyment of doing business.

- A leaders' role is in envisioning the future which demands purity of mind. Visionaries use the mind for its primary purpose, for deep thinking and developing ideas.

"

Keep your mind pure.
Purity of mind defines your
leadership capacity.

"

Being focused is putting your strengths forward. Lack of focus means putting your blind spots forward. Lack of focus leads to only one scenario – failure.

FOCUS

Fishing demands all your focus.

It was such a beautiful Saturday that I decided to skip all my city hassle and go fishing. It was absolutely logical – fresh salmon runs into a river and wouldn't catch itself, whereas business and home things could wait till after the weekend. A perfect day at the peak of the season does not happen often while shelves can be cleaned any day.

I jumped in my car and was fishing exactly at the time a fresh school of salmon came into the river. However, I still blamed myself for not doing things I planned to do and started calling partners and colleagues whilst casting.

In a middle of a call, I had a sudden strike and reflexively made a step backward, on a small slippery stone. The next moment I was under the water. The fish was lost, I was wet, and my friend who stood nearby sarcastically noted, "I love how you artistically play the role of Poseidon rising from the water, angry and wet."

I checked my rod and felt that something was missing. Here I realized that my shiny new phone that cost a ton of money went as a bribe to the fish. Why did I take a phone with me wading into a river? Why do I need a phone when fishing? Did nature take revenge for me losing focus? The result was costly – phone, fish, and a lost day of fishing as I couldn't carry on being soaked.

Focus is like a fishing line that connects us with the fish, it directly connects us to what we aim to achieve. Focus is a tool that makes the distance to success shorter and more achievable.

When we lose focus, we lose connection, we lose thought, and we lose energy for doing important things. We lose ourselves. By losing focus, we are consciously or unconsciously making success harder to achieve.

In leadership, the focus is a central point of attention that pulls the effort of all involved in execution together and defines the deliverables. It must be appealing to all to maintain the will to execute. The leader's role is to maintain the team's focus.

LESSONS LEARNED:

- Being focused is putting your strengths forward. Lack of focus means putting your blind spots forward. Lack of focus leads to only one scenario – failure.

- If a leader promised people that they would achieve something great then he or she has to help them stay focused on it. In their turn, people will be focused on a vision and exercise a strong will to make it a reality if they see these qualities in their leader.

- Being focused means making rational use of resources for the achievement of this goal. A team with a focused understanding of a goal understands the resources it will require.

- Those with a strong focus and a will to win become winners, those without focus and a will to win have already lost.

- Think pragmatically about how much a loss of focus costs you and your business, in monetary terms. Don't be shocked when you see those digits.

"

If something goes wrong,
then pause to make it right.
If you don't have good options,
don't do bad options.

PAUSE TO WIN

Salmon fishing is very much about that moment of sensation when the fish is hooked on the fly. All fishermen get caught in the anticipation – the heart is pumping, muscles shiver in anticipation of a powerful take, adrenalin is produced in gallons, and nerves are tense. It will happen now, in a couple of casts, very soon... Then...nothing happens.

I have experience catching salmon at the first few casts or even on the first cast. Unfortunately, in most cases, this is a game of patience and anticipation.

The more desperate I am to hook a fish, the less the chances are. It took me a few years to realize this simple axiom. It took even longer to accept it consciously.

I was once in such a rush to catch a fish I almost killed all the joy in the experience. Time flew by and I didn't have even a gentle touch to my bait. The more I cast, the more I was sucked into despair. Success moved further away with my every cast.

I don't know why and how but a simple thought came across my mind – stop being so desperate like you have nothing to eat at home and this is the only chance to feed my family. Relax and enjoy this terrific process.

I waded out of the water, put my rod down, and comfortably relaxed. I recalled similar days and found a pattern of five strong signals to take a break that I ignored before.

The first signal – If a fish doesn't take for a long while, stop casting, sit and relax, give the pool time to relax, and meanwhile rethink how to attract the fish. Fish ignore me for a reason. Pause to think twice before acting. Fish are there which meant I was doing something wrong – pause and think again.

The second signal – Fish don't look for a fisherman, a fisherman must find fish. Honestly, I fished a few times in pools with no fish in them, which I realized too late. Salmon is not where it is comfortable for me, but where it is good for salmon. I must pause and evaluate, and move to another pool if needed.

The third signal – My thoughts are not on fishing. In other words, I wasn't present and was unconsciously doing something wrong. If I can't feel myself, how can I feel the environment and find fish? Being detached from the present is a sin in fishing.

The fourth signal – I was rushing too much which led to mistakes. As a result, the fish is spooked, and I continue micromanaging the process, making it worse. Spooking fish by bombarding it with your casts only does harm.

The fifth signal is simple physical and/or psychological exhaustion. Fishing is about energy and positivity. If I don't have physical and psychological energy, then I can't be effective.

These five signals are very relevant to leadership.

Corporate life hijacks our consciousness, clouds our minds, and even our ability to pause when needed by pushing us non-stop. We desperately need lucid moments to calm down and have clarity before acting.

Success is not granted for nothing. It comes to those who are prepared, which takes time. If you don't have good options or opportunities, it doesn't mean you should continue by doing something wrong.

Waiting and pausing is not losing. It is a sign of maturity and approaching something challenging by being conscious. Only in Westerns do cowboys draw their guns without thinking.

We need to pause to get insights from nature when fishing. We need to pause to get insights from the market reality when in business.

The sensation of hooking a fish is born in the pause before casting. We need to pause to gain a bigger view of where and how we will fish for success.

LESSONS LEARNED:

- The ability to pause and knowing when to pause is a sign of a strong leader who cares about good preparation. Weak leaders tend to jump the gun; strong leaders pause to think.

- The inability to pause leads to stress and ineffectiveness. Burnout is costly.

- By not pausing, we tend to regress into micromanagement.

- Pausing is needed for the conscious decision to foresee, invite, and embrace a forthcoming success. Rushing pushes success further away. Despair blinds.

- If something goes wrong, then pause to make it right. If you don't have good options, don't do bad options.

- Stress is the result of not understanding what you are doing.

"

By not pausing, we tend to regress into micromanagement.

CONVERSATIONS AROUND THE CAMPFIRE

"

If you've ever been around a group of actors,
you've noticed, no doubt, that they can talk of
nothing else under the sun but acting.
It's exactly the same way with baseball players.
Your heart must be in your work.

Christy Mathewson

"

*Noise attracts attention,
a quiet voice opens hearts.*

BROTHERS IN RODS AND FORKS

Fly fishermen share the same syndrome, "fishocardia" which is caused by addiction to something greater than just a hobby and makes every fisherman's heartbeat many times faster when a fish is sensed. Fly fishing is a lifestyle in which rank, titles, or wealth are not important. They all have that unique gene in their DNA.

When we go fishing in good company, this is already something to appreciate and celebrate. Good fishing buddies have a principle – catch together, cook together, and eat together.

We catch together. Salmon fishing is very much the result of collective knowledge. We learn from each other to become professionals. No one can become a professional on his own and in such a complicated art as fly fishing.

Whether two or three or four of us are off together after salmon, it is always meticulously perfect teamwork. We share loads, exchange flies and contribute to each other without saying much. I've tied countless flies for my friends for granted.

Of course, we are in some kind of competition on who gets more fish or will catch the largest one. At the same time, we help each other to find and catch fish. Something like, "I saw a nice fish there. This is your fish" can be heard all the time.

There are days when salmon ignore everything. This becomes a challenge for all and if one of us catches a fish, we celebrate together. This is a common understanding – "A salmon he caught made my day. His win is mine as well, and I celebrate it." We are Brothers in Rods supporting and celebrating each other.

We cook together. Nothing can beat wild salmon caught just an hour before cooked on a campfire. It is something beyond delicious – tender, juicy, and with a vivid flavor. This is simply a Michelin chef's dream. It is enriched with woody smoke and freshly ground spices. It is something divine.

Now add to this a lot of jokes and a ton of laughter in a setting more beautiful than most people can even imagine. This is a feast that the gods of Olympus would be jealous of.

We don't talk much during fishing. Sharing this feast is a time for heart-to-heart conversation and faces that shine with positivity from within. We love each other. True Brothers in Forks.

No politics, purely sharing emotions, fishing stories, and experiences, and multiplying each other's passion.

Noise attracts attention, a quiet voice opens hearts. We noticed that no one raises their voice in such conversations, even when debating over what fly is the best. We talk meaningfully in low voices. Our minds and hearts are open and receptive. This is something that can't be seen in the office.

The outcome is all of us being infused with positivity, unforgettable experiences, and new knowledge. We become a Brotherhood in Rods and Forks.

I believe that nature makes us better listeners and communicators. Nature connects people.

LESSONS LEARNED:

- Let your people be co-owners of success by contributing to it and benefiting from it and learning from each other.

- I have a simple principle in life and in business – if we cook together, we eat together. This allows for strong partnerships.

- An ability to join resources connects our humanity. The same with creating a strong team – as a leader, encourage members to join their resources to become better.

- Noise attracts attention, a quiet voice opens hearts.

- A compelling leadership vision is a strong emotion in itself. It makes people passionate. These emotions drive people to put themselves through anything uncomfortable and challenging to executing a vision.

"

*Let your people be co-owners
of success by contributing to it
and benefiting from it
and learning from each other.*

A CEO WITH A FLY ROD – KRIS KLEIN

Talking to someone who travels the world fishing whilst running the company that every fly fisherman respects greatly is something special.

Kris Klein is the CEO of Sage, a producer of the world's finest performance fly rods and reels. Kris fishes the world, not just travels it.

> "Fishing in general, makes all of us more connected to the world. There is no greater or grander connection in the world than fishing. It is something that requires a lifelong pursuit to be good at it and it is extremely challenging.
>
> This is an eternal pursuit of learning. I've spent time with some of the world's greatest anglers and each one of them still talks about things that they have to continue to learn and grow. I am the CEO of a world-renowned fly-fishing company and I feel like an amateur most days in what I'm doing.
>
> This is life's purpose; to recognize that we are just very small pieces of a very large world. We have so much to continue to evolve and grow into and candidly, give back.

I remember standing in the Big Wood River which is a river outside Sun Valley, Idaho, and had a spectacular day of fishing. I was standing in the stream and looking over just off to my left, and there's this trout. Looking up at me, it came up, took a fly right off the surface, dove deep down, and looked back up at me and just kind of kept sitting right in that same feed line. I watched this fish for about 15 minutes and it was one of the most amazing connections that I've ever had.

I travel a lot, which provides the opportunity for one to get out and about and meet people all over the world, being able to experience the world's cultures and learn different life perspectives. There's so much variety and distinction between fishing in Alaska and spending time with people in Brazil when fishing there. When two anglers meet each other, they always have something to talk about. This is about fishing and how passionate they are regardless of what kind of fish they are chasing. This is a power of passion that bonds different people into one brotherhood.

Fishing is about giving back, to people and to the community. As a leader, one of my roles is to inspire and grow others. Ultimately, I must be very good at sharing passion and pulling young people into the organization by teaching them how to learn and what to learn. This is one of the greatest gifts and joys, getting people to learn things and develop shared knowledge with others.

Fishing is about being able to understand and read circumstances and situations and infer from not only what you see but what you feel, and what you might be able to gather from others. Fishing is more about EQ than IQ.

Fishing is about patience. Patience makes you stop, listen, observe, and learn. It does set you up though, for the ability to look and see things holistically as opposed to specifically and keep your point. I think there are many technical aspects in the fly-fishing space, which means

I understand the grain weight of a line, I understand how many wraps are in a fly, and so on. Yet, fishing is about understanding how to spend time with people and understand what's going on in circumstances and how to pursue the situation. It may not be about this cast and maybe about the forecast ahead of being, that's what's important.

As a CEO, fishing taught me to be in pursuit of becoming better as a human, how to accelerate my ability to communicate with different people, have a holistic view of circumstances and events, develop my EQ, constantly learn and refresh my skillset, be comfortable being uncomfortable, stretch myself to be better, be resilient, remain authentic, and be grateful to people and the world."

Thank you, Kris, for sharing your passion and wisdom.

TALKING TO LORI AMES, A FISHERWOMAN WITH A GREAT PASSION

There is a common belief that fishing is predominantly for men. This is totally wrong! I have met so many women passionate about fishing and often more successful than men in catching trophies.

Lori Ames is an amazing publicist from New York, founder and President of ThePRFreelancer, Inc. She has a passion for making business authors stand out six days a week. Yet, every Tuesday, Lori is out fishing.

> "Fishing and business, or business and fishing. After my family, these are my two favorite things.
>
> There are many corollaries between fishing and running a business – patience, tenacity, lows and highs, creativity, and adapting.

Fishing and being a mom have both taught me patience. As a recreational fisherwoman, I tend to go once a week from May through the beginning of October.

TALKING TO LORI AMES, A FISHERWOMAN WITH A GREAT PASSION

You don't catch a fish every time out so you learn to enjoy the air, the water, and the company of others. In business, patience is so important when working with new employees, new clients, and dealing with the uncertainty of sales funnels, cash flow, pandemics, and other unpredictable crises.

Patience and tenacity go hand in hand in fishing and business. When I first fished for striped bass, I went five weeks in a row without a bite; on week six I caught two. I was determined that eventually, I would master the technique... and I did!

In business, that's comparable to writing proposals. Not every proposal is going to turn into a client project but you can't give up. Entrepreneurship is not about the overnight success stories that make headlines. Entrepreneurship, leadership, small business success is all about patience and tenacity, and learning as you go.

Lows and highs in fishing lead to great catches and tremendous disappointments, especially when you are reeling in what feels like a super nice-sized fish and then it breaks off (if you watch *Wicked Tuna* you'll know what I mean).

My fishing is on a much lower scale than that but when you have something on the line, and you're reeling it in, the adrenaline starts pumping. When it breaks off there's usually a little cursing involved. In business, it's actually quite similar. You have your new business call and are excited about a new project, you write your proposal, you follow up, you answer more questions, and then...sometimes the prospect says, 'Sorry, we decided to go another direction,' which is a nice way of saying that you lost out to the fisherman on the other side of the boat. Adrenaline followed by a letdown. But you move forward and rebait your hook and drop back down in the water...there's always another fish there, just sometimes not right away.

There are no magic wands in fishing or business, but I keep them on my desk and around my office anyway. Creativity in fishing you may ask? Everyone has their favorite rig, lure, rod, and reel...some have their favorite hat. It's a form of creativity. Creativity in business helps you think broader, solve problems, and develop new revenue streams.

TALKING TO LORI AMES, A FISHERWOMAN WITH A GREAT PASSION

Adapting is key to everything in life. On the water we have to adapt to wind, tide, rain, sun, and sometimes the people fishing next to us who are just learning and tangle our lines.

In business, we have to adapt to industry changes, consumer changes, AI, ChatGPT, and supply chain issues. But giving up is not an option. I started my business under the worst of circumstances...from my son's Neuro ICU room; I was trying to create a semblance of normalcy in a situation that had nothing normal about it. A dozen years later and he's thriving and so is my business. You can't give up and you can't listen to the naysayers. You need to adapt to catch that keeper fish for dinner as well as to build a successful business."

Talking to Lori, I learned a few things:

- Catching a trophy in business and in fishing demands very similar qualities of a leader.

- Passion for leadership and for fishing doesn't have gender or nationality. A true passion is evident in any who put their heart into something beyond their own self.

- Creativity is an enhanced form of passion.

TALKING TO JOHN SPENCE, A TOP LEADERSHIP EXPERT CASTING FOR TROUT

Countless times, I've talked about fishing with my old friend John Spence. He also co-authored *Mind Crafting* with me. John is one of the world's top business and leadership experts. He's also a fanatical fisherman. He grew up in Florida and spent summers chasing marlins in the Bahamas. Later in life, he switched to fly fishing for trout. When he's not in a corporate board room or giving a speech to 10,000 people, you can usually find him standing in a river.

> "Fishing helped to make my life and leadership more meaningful. It's not about catching fish. There is so much more to it. Preparing your tackle and lures. Studying the map looking for the best spots. Driving to where there are no other cars and then walking for miles to that piece of the river you have been dreaming about. Hours spent working the river. Casting thousands of times. Not catching a single fish yet marking the day as one of the best in your life. It's about the process, not the outcome.

I don't know if it has made me any wiser, but I'm definitely more thoughtful. Being alone on the river with only my thoughts for company gives me time for reflection. The babble of the stream washes away worry and restlessness. Fresh air clears my mind. Time slows down and allows me to ponder life's big questions. It is as though the stream is fishing for ideas from me.

I'm learning as a leader every time I fish, waist deep in a rushing river, slowly walking across slippery rocks. Casting a long line to a small fish with a tiny fly. This requires absolute focus. To me, it is the same in business and leadership. Focusing your team on a compelling vision. Creating a strategy to achieve that vision. Working diligently towards the vision. Looking carefully for opportunities. Steering clear of dangers. Constantly moving forward. On the river and in your life, it's about focus, patience, and diligence."

John, thank you for your wisdom – success starts before the start. If a leader is fully prepared, attuned, and focused, then he gains, learns, and wins.

TALKING TO CARMEL DE NAHLIK, A SOLUTION FINDER WHO MEDIATES EVEN WITH FISH

I talked with Carmel de Nahlik, who has spent a lifetime sorting out sensitive complex problems and is now a mediator in the West Midlands, UK.

Carmel spoke of the similarities between mediation and problem-solving and fishing. Mediation requires the same sense of calm that is important when approaching a river or the sea and the same sense of awareness of the conditions and the environment.

The mediator is an enabler and observer, making small adjustments and replaying what has been said, just like casting and fly selection.

During a mediation, the mediator has to have that same sense of flow that we mentioned and mastery to be able to improvise and identify solutions that will work for all and that may be outside the prescribed and accepted norm. Patience is very important at what may be an emotional time for those describing difficult situations. Building trust is also important and that requires investment of time and know-how.

TALKING TO CARMEL DE NAHLIK, A SOLUTION FINDER WHO MEDIATES EVEN WITH FISH

Finally, sometimes the fish gets away and the mediation or difficulty is not resolved. Just as in the fishing stories, you need to pick yourself up and move on.

"Many years ago, I was an impoverished student and used to visit the Scilly Isles, just off the coast of Cornwall with a friend. At that time, there was not a well-developed tourist infrastructure and the economy was going through a very difficult time with prices rising very steeply. We couldn't afford to shop much at the single island shop, so we brought dried soya protein with us and planned to catch fish to supplement our diet. We were both new to sea fishing and indeed to fishing completely having had a five-minute tutorial in the shop while buying the cheapest tackle we could afford. We knew other campers like us caught fish because they had boats and would often generously share any excess with us. But we needed to catch our own and we were told we could fish from the cliffs. So off we set, intent on mackerel, or even pollock, both delicious fish. We had no proper bait, other than some stinky whiting that we had been given.

We chose a spot on the cliff and I cast what seemed like a very long way down, probably about 20 to 30 feet. The bait was taken very quickly and I was looking forward to roast fish that evening. However, the fish had other ideas. Quickly moving to an area where the rocks had been eroded under the waterline, I tugged on the line and so did the fish, using the rocks as leverage and almost pulling me in. Eventually a tired fisher and fish managed to meet and back to camp we went.

The fish was a wrasse, a very beautiful golden fish and naïvely we assumed that we would just scale it. Wrong. The wrasse had skin like sandpaper and after considerable shedding of blood we managed to clean and cook it and sat down to eat it, to discover that after our efforts, there was very little substance to it and a lot of bones. We retired mostly hungry.

Here I learned that sometimes, size is immaterial, using the environment can offer small entities considerable leverage. It pays to do the environmental research – we had the wrong bait for the fish we wanted and we hadn't considered the risks of fishing off a steep cliff. We also didn't know what a wrasse was. Acquisition targets can look beautiful, delicious and wonderful and turn out to be thin on valuable resources. Is the effort worth it?

TALKING TO CARMEL DE NAHLIK, A SOLUTION FINDER WHO MEDIATES EVEN WITH FISH

Fly fishing for trout taught me a lot. My first encounter with fly fishing was joining a family of keen fisherfolk. But I couldn't catch a fish. I cast efficiently, I had the right fly, the leader floated, and the fish ignored it. It took about 18 months to catch my first fish, bearing in mind limited access to the river.

On one summer's day, just after I got married, I was in a state of flow, and landed a large wild brown trout. I'm still not sure which of us was more surprised. My next experience was a single visit fishing for wild fish with an untamed bank and a population of very shy trout and grayling. Again, I was fortunate, and both catches were delicious.

In my opinion, a state of flow is really important for success, whatever the context. When things come together subconsciously, actions are almost seamless and success is guaranteed.

To get there requires a lot of practice and rehearsal and those are the things that many people do not see. Acquiring that knowledge enables you to be able to put it into practice without thinking. But that investment is never recovered and needs to be honored and acknowledged as part of your good practice as a successful leader.

I had an interesting experience. It was the last day of the season and almost the last hour before we would go home, a drive of several hundred miles. I had one fly left in my box that was the guaranteed winner every time, so I cast it and of course, it got caught in a small tree.

Here I must note that I was heavily pregnant at the time when our daughter arrived about a month later. Tired and grumpy, I wrenched at the tree, the fly and the leader came free with the line and physics dictated action and reaction so into the river I went. I had never really thought about this very beautiful stream. The waters were clear, the fish were present but I hadn't thought about how deep it was, or considered that I was fishing on a bend. Down I went, waters closing over my head, up I came eventually spitting out water and trying to get to the bank but of course, the weight was all in the wrong place. Eventually, I managed to get out to see an anxious husband running down the bank.

TALKING TO CARMEL DE NAHLIK, A SOLUTION FINDER WHO MEDIATES EVEN WITH FISH

It was getting dark, I was soaked, and it was getting cold, we had a long walk back to the fishing hut where our main possessions were and an even longer walk to the car. So back to the hut we squelched, changed clothes, and off to the car trudged my husband just about decently clad in waterproofs. Without any fish. With lots of tests for various waterborne diseases."

Later, thinking of this experience, I realized a few lessons.

- Be patient – a fit of pique can undermine all that hard work in a moment.

- There is always another day. Time pressures may be perceived rather than real.

- Again, it's always important to understand the environment and to invest time in really looking at what is going on and adapting to the specific circumstances. Also, one of the key rules of mediation – always "read the room."

Thank you so much for your invaluable lessons, dear Carmel. I'm always your grateful student.

DAVID MATTSON, A CEO IN WADERS

Running a global business and being a keen fly fisherman is not for a faint hearted or shallow-thinking personality. I talked to David Mattson about his leadership lessons from fishing.

David Mattson is the CEO and President of Sandler Training from Maryland, United States. David is a best-selling author, sales and management thought leader, keynote speaker, and leader for sales training seminars around the world. As CEO and President of Sandler Training, David oversees the corporate direction and strategy for the company's global operations including sales, marketing, consulting, alliances, and support.

> "Fishing makes me wiser. Because you're looking outward and you're also looking inward and that makes me wise.

You have to read the environment but you also have to change what you're doing and I think that that connection between internal and external is huge. Fishing makes me wiser because you have to be self-accountable, and you have to be flexible.

Fishing is very much about nuances as we know little about the drift and what is going on underwater. I must pay attention to many things and be generally correct, yet still miss the mark.

I can't change what is going on there but I can change how I think and what I do. People often say that small nuances don't really matter. In my view, a lot of little things make a big thing.

This is like in business – why did you buy from this company even though their product costs more? The answer is that there is a connection there. There are nuances you had the same products and the same pricing model, but below the water things actually happened that I think people don't pay attention to. So, I think from that perspective, it makes you wiser.

I think it also makes me wiser because of my forward thinking. You don't look straight down when you fish, you look out and I think that makes you wiser as you look at the horizon of life and the horizon in the business community versus what's going on right now in my world. You have to look out and look at that bigger picture, be a decision-maker, and rely on your own intuition and your learnings.

Also, you can be fishing with friends, but you're by yourself for the most part which makes you wiser because I'm not relying on everyone telling me what to do. I've got to figure it out and the ultimate way, it makes me wiser is that I learned by failure as much as I learned by success. 'What did I learn from that? What am I going to do differently? What did work and can you repeat it?' This approach makes you really wise.

Being wise is also about being adaptive. It's that flexibility within the margin because if you're not allowing yourself this flexibility you will be stuck with the same fly, with the same cast, whatever you will be banging the same pool with no result. Leaders must be adaptive.

Fishing is a never-ending process of learning about yourself. One day, I went into one of my favorite streams and I think I have picked the right spot, but I'm not catching anything.

I started to believe it was not true, maybe that was a bad spot, maybe there was no fish and I listed all the environmental reasons including barometric pressure. There's got to be a million reasons. So, it cannot be me. It must not be me. I obviously have picked a worse spot in this river. I looked downriver and saw people catching fish.

I became angry at myself. What just happened was because of me, not the environment. There's actually fish here. Then a light bulb went on and I took a deep breath and thought about what I haven't done. I probably didn't change the way, I probably didn't change my fly often enough, I probably didn't do X & Y.

You have a whole list of other things that could potentially work. But without me seeing them, I would get caught in my own externalization that it's everything but me. Wisdom and life lessons that we have go out the window until we see that reflective mirror that shows a need to change the mindset and change behavior. Mindset and behavior are that combination of success which is more probable, but I was only focused on really the technique part, and it wasn't working.

I learned that when walking into the water for fishing, always leave your ego on the bank.

We tend to believe that the grass is greener on the other side. Or, there's always going to be a better deal somewhere else. In fact, there's always going to be you, your mindset, and your behavior. You have to go in with an open mind because you can only control your own behaviors. You can't control the environment. If you don't control your own behaviors, the environment will eat you. That's probably the best lesson that I can take into my business world and into my life.

Fishing is a mindset game. You always have to ask why – why are they doing this, or why is this happening, what's this like, why is the river doing 'X'?

In our business approach, we have something that's called the success triangle. When we teach people about sales, it has attitude, behavior, and technique. Most often, people want the technique, how do I cast better? Okay, that's fine. But this will never make anyone a great leader. You're never going to be a great salesperson. You'll never be a great parent. You'll never be a great fisherman because you need the mindset and introspection, and behaviors, whether in fishing or in leadership.

Fishing is a continuous journey and you can never be satisfied with what you know today because it's not going to be the same tomorrow and as much as I think I've conquered parts of my business life."

David, thank you for sharing your wisdom. Whether in fishing or in leadership, success is about mindset and behavior coming first and techniques after.

APPRECIATION FOR GROWTH

"

*When I started counting my blessings,
my whole life turned around.*

Willie Nelson

"

*Leadership is defined
by the reasons
people stand by your side.*

PERSONALITY TO EXPLORE AND FALL IN LOVE WITH

It is impossible to know the world by looking at it through a window or on TV. We can explore the world only when stepping over the doorstep and determining to experience it.

An old Lapland fisherman said to me when we chatted over tea made from wild berries on a campfire, "Every river has its character and voice. Listen to it and you will never forget it."

I fished in Scotland, Iceland, Norway, and Russia – Nith, Swarta, Blanda, Pasvik, Kola, Zapadnaya Litza, Ura, and Umba, to name a few. Exploring these gems of nature by blazing along, I fall in love with every river. Meeting a new river is meeting a new personality. It roars at you at the beginning, then you learn about it, and then you become friends. I understood more about the river's personality when walking along it. I fell in love with them, got to know them, was able to catch more fish, and learned more about myself.

I can't forget the Icelandic rivers. Swarta (Black River) is a small river in the North of Iceland that bears its name because of the black volcanic sand on its bed that makes crystal clear water look black or dark. It is a black pearl of Iceland's rivers. Swarta falls into a larger river, Blanda (White River) which has unusual milky-colored water flowing strongly from glaciers showing its Viking personality.

I love the rivers of the Arctic, of the land of the midnight sun where shadows are horizontal and changes are unpredictable. Long and broad Kola, the river with a big personality legendary for its exemplary big salmon. Zapadnaya Litza taught me many lessons showing its untamed personality with every waterfall and rocky stretches. Ura is a small crystal-water river that may look shy and small, yet it holds so many secrets and many rewards and gifts if you know it well. Ura is my most beloved river.

Every river stretches for many kilometers flowing through rocks, woods, shallows, canyons, long calm stretches flowing low and high, and taking in the tides. Every river is living, dynamic, and relentless.

I was skeptical about that old Lapland man's insight until I explored more and fell in love with rivers. They talk, they feel, they respond, they reward and punish, and they live. Just listen to them as they have a lot to share.

PERSONALITY TO EXPLORE AND FALL IN LOVE WITH

By exploring rivers' personalities, I became adept at noticing little changes that make big differences in fishing – water level, speed and pressure of the flow, temperature changes, the color of the water, sunny or overcast weather, and many other things. Being grounded in the reality of now and envisioning forthcoming changes which in human terms can be viewed as what mood the river is and how it will behave soon.

I must explore the personality of the river myself. I can't become friends with something or someone so important based on the stories of others. The same in leadership. As a leader, I must explore my people to love them and do my best for them. No formal report can help with this. I must learn to see the beauty of nature and the world to be able to see the beauty in people.

No one rules nature. Nature generously rewards those who are immersed in and become a part of it. You are either a grateful guest or a parasite. Similarly, a leader is not a ruler but a grateful servant who knows people well. No leader can be involved, empathetic, and truly connected if he or she doesn't know their own people. You must know people to love them and serve them best as a leader.

LESSONS LEARNED:

- Leadership is defined by the reasons people stand by your side.

- You can't help people to grow and achieve something great without knowing them. A leader must be truly connected and involved with people in order to reveal their superpowers. Explore your people and you will discover a huge, grateful universe.

- Reliance on formal reports closes doors to people's hearts. Only direct interaction allows shared affection and engagement.

- You wouldn't pollute a river you love. You wouldn't be toxic with people you love.

- Swarta brings its black waters into the milky-white waters of Blanda making it stronger and full of fish. Diversity is the same. We need diverse people to make a team stronger and more resourceful.

"

You wouldn't pollute a river you love. You wouldn't be toxic with people you love.

"

No challenge is given beyond our capacity to withstand it. Simply get the extra strength from nature.

THE HEALER

The largest and strongest salmon come in the rivers at the very beginning of the season when the arctic rivers are just cleared from ice, and the water is still freezing cold. Fish come in small schools making their way to spawning grounds far upstream.

The metabolism of salmon is very low in such cold water and they hardly respond to flies, making them difficult to catch. Yet, every fisherman dreams about fighting a giant, and I'm not an exception.

I cast for a few hours standing waist-deep in a stream of +4C water without any luck. My enthusiasm melted down and only that strong desire to catch a dream fish made me continue. I danced on my toes to warm up and fell into the water, of course. Carelessness is punished.

I quickly changed my clothing and continued not feeling very comfortable but eager to continue. Yet, very quickly, I gave up and went home. I focused on myself and my comfort and not on the challenge.

At the end of the same year, a couple of days before Christmas, I was driving around Rovaniemi, the capital of Santa Claus. The weather was fairly Christmassy – a few snowflakes, and a breathtaking -35C.

Suddenly, I noticed a tiny lemming crossing a snowy road and promptly disappeared into the snow on the other side of the road. This was something mystical to me.

How does such a small and defenseless creature, the size of a matchbox, without fangs and warm fur, survive in such harsh conditions? And this little creature is important for nature!

Seeing this lemming and its resilience made me think from a different perspective – not about my own comfort but about resilience within the context of a greater environment. I'm a part of nature and nothing beyond my capability would be given to me.

Later in the day, sipping coffee in a nice roadside coffee shop accompanied by "Jingle Bells," I connected these two seemingly distant events in my mind and realized that I could learn from them and use them in practice. Not just to be a cog in some mindless, soulless machine, but to understand who I am and what to do.

THE HEALER

I was thinking about myself when I fell into the cold water and was thinking about my being a part of nature when I observed the lemming.

We all face tough situations when our inner gremlins take control. When I'm closed from within and defending myself, when I desperately need more positive energy, I continue basking in poisonous thoughts.

However, when I open my heart and mind to the vast beauty of the world and embrace life instead of defending a little space called "myself," I allow positive energy to flow effortlessly through me. Seeing myself as a part of nature makes me powerful and resilient.

Nature has taught me to be kind to myself but without pity. The lemming certainly does not know what self-pity is and lives contentedly.

Nature is like a healer that enhances the immune system, improving your ability to handle stress. We often see our problems as the size of a huge airship, and nature helps us see that they are the size of a kid's balloon, and we ourselves hold it in our hands. This leads to losing ourselves.

Throughout my life, I've had great wins and sad losses. I learned something very important – I can lose everything but must never lose myself.

Nature is a charging station of energy and consciousness that gives me freedom of thought and provides a greater view of life. This is not about always winning but standing up and bouncing forward in tough times as a manifestation of my natural authenticity.

Nature is the greatest healer of our inner wounds that gives strength and courage to continue.

LESSONS LEARNED:

- Nature helps to clear the mind and see through the uncertainty of our psychological wounds whilst molding us into a stronger version of ourselves.

THE HEALER

- Without nature, we are only slightly different from the advanced version of AI which is fed on electricity. We desperately need feelings, emotions, passion, and our own authenticity that nature gives us.

- No challenge is given beyond our capacity to withstand it. Simply get the extra strength from nature.

- The understanding of being an important part of something huge as nature or the universe makes you stronger.

- Due to our hectic lives, we lose peace and passion for life itself. Nature has peace and a passion for life in abundance. You just need to turn to this source of vitality and come out strong and resilient.

"

Care for nature is a reinforced investment in the well-being of the next generations.

TAKE CARE OF THE ENVIRONMENT THAT TAKES CARE OF YOU AND YOUR CHILDREN

We all win having nature clean. City dwellers, regardless of intention, have at best an intellectual understanding of this. When interacting with nature directly, we feel it in our bones.

In the tundra, where everything grows very slowly and nature is very fragile, it takes about twenty years for the trail of a Caterpillar all-terrain vehicle to be overgrown. In fact, the marks remain visible for many years, like old wounds on the body of a soldier. A pioneer is someone who sees potential even in such lifeless surroundings.

It isn't easy keeping the ocean clean. All trawlers lose gear and most of it is plastic, which will be a risk to sea life for centuries.

We found metal jars made in the 40s which are still in good shape. Glass will stay forever. Every piece of plastic, glass, or aluminum left on a river bank or in a forest is an artifact of our carelessness for future generations. Do we want our children and grandchildren to inherit waste? I want my son to enjoy nature as I do.

My friend, Igor calls all wild creatures "forest brothers." We have our own rules for taking care of them. Take everything that is left over from our dining back home, except fresh vegetables that lemmings, minks, stoats, and other little brothers love so much. Watching a funny little mink stealing and chewing a cucumber is such a joy.

We always have special bags for a simple purpose – to take away the trash we find. Cleaning around us is a matter of respect for nature. It takes minutes, yet improves things for years. We thoroughly cleaned one of our beloved fishing spots, and a week later we found a lot of birds, foxes, and other little animals' footprints on the sand that we never saw there before.

We are nature's dependents; nature is not dependent on humans. A responsible person should leave nature pristine. We are not users, but guardians of nature. Leave the environment cleaner than before you came to it. Nature doesn't pollute people. People pollute nature.

Keeping nature clean is a message from your heart, "Nature, I love you and am grateful for your gifts!"

TAKE CARE OF THE ENVIRONMENT THAT TAKES CARE OF YOU AND YOUR CHILDREN

The corporate world is obsessed with mission statements and loud declarations of sustainability and environmental protection. This is great. However, sustainability and legacy are not in the declaration but in action.

LESSONS LEARNED:

- A harmful footprint puts your children's interaction with nature on pause or destroys it completely.

- A father of a house is responsible for it and the surrounding area as well. A leader is responsible for having his or her organization's environment clean.

- Think how much it will cost the next generations to clean nature after you fish or simply have a barbecue there.

- Nature is not a free shop, but an area of responsibility that begins at the leader's desk.

- Care for nature is a reinforced investment in the well-being of the next generations.

"

*Fishing is a labor of love.
Leadership is a labor of love.
Love and care are my tackle to
catch people's hearts and minds.*

PUTTING RODS AWAY AFTER THE SEASON

The season ends, yet life continues and new seasons are ahead of us. Putting your rods away after the season is a great moment to sit with a nice cup of coffee or whiskey and reflect through incredible moments of interacting with nature and thinking of preparing for the next season.

Fishing is not about fish. It is about interacting with nature and learning from it. Nature is the wisest leadership coach available and helps one to become better with every interaction. Nature is a source, not a resource. A moment of connection with nature leads to the realization of your inner strengths.

Success in fishing comes when you become a part of nature, not a mere visitor. Success with people comes when you are a part of them and create value for them every day. Casting for fish we are revealing ourselves and learning about life and leadership where every cast is not into the water but into the core of ourselves.

Living in an era of AI we neglect the fact that no AI can beat or will ever change the emotions and feelings of a human that is connected with nature. We train AI to think like a human, but we can't train AI to think and be emotional.

We will have driverless cars, but we will never have people-less organizations. Nature helps us to remain human and to learn about others in an authentic environment. This is what AI can't do.

A modern leader must be book-wise, street-wise, and nature-wise. Books teach us about facts, phenomena, events, and other interesting things. Being street-wise helps us to communicate with people effectively. Being nature-wise makes us mature, true to ourselves and others, and teaches things not in any book.

Every fishing trip is transformational. Every leadership task is transformational. Every interaction with nature, every interaction with people, every challenge, and every moment of exploring something new is a moment of transformation if we are prepared to open our minds and hearts. Lose yourself in nature to find yourself. Lose yourself in this abundance to realize an abundance within you.

Albert Einstein said, "There are two ways to live: as if nothing is a miracle, or as if everything is a miracle." Fishing is about discovering a miracle in nature, in life, and in people.

Fishing helps me to enhance my humility and keeps my ego on a short leash – on every trip I have questions to explore. It shows that I know little or even nothing and must learn more. There is always something to learn as no one can wade into the same river twice. I'm an eternal student of nature.

Constant learning is the norm allowing you to see the beauty of the world – the forces of nature, millions of colors, unpredictable changes, and incredible people with whom and for whom you work. Whether in fishing or in leadership, mastery is defined by the ability to learn, unlearn, and learn again. If you can't do this, then don't try to pretend.

We all have limited resources. At the same time, we all have an abundance of resources around us. Leadership is about learning how to behold the abundance. Thus, you learn to be ready for changes and challenges at any moment and have everything you need at hand.

Regardless of what stage of leadership you are at, a novice needing guidance, a pirate that has already crossed the ocean a couple of times, a strategist, or even a visionary leader, remember that leadership is a privilege. Being a leader is not a rank or position. This is a credit from people that is due every day. Learn how to repay it with the most value for people.

Fishing is a labor of love. Leadership is a labor of love. Love and care are my tackle to catch people's hearts and minds.

ABOUT THE AUTHOR

Dr. Oleg Konovalov is a global thought leader, author, business educator, consultant, and C-suite coach.

Oleg is named among the top eight global experts in leadership and shortlisted for the Distinguished Award in Leadership by Thinkers50 (2021). He is on Global Gurus Top 30 in Leadership, is the #1 Global Leading Coach (Marshall Goldsmith Thinkers50 Award), and has been named one of the Global 100 Inspirational Leaders 2022, along with Bill Gates, Elon Musk, Jeff Bezos, and Oprah Winfrey.

Having been named "the da Vinci of Visionary Leadership" by many leading authorities of our time, Oleg is considered #1 in the world in the field of vision and visionary leadership.

He is the author of *The Vision Code*, *Leaderology*, and other books.

www.olegkonovalov.com

Oleg Konovalov video course, *How to Create a Strong Vision for Life and Business*

Made in the USA
Middletown, DE
18 February 2024